A
Shared
Vision

Education in Church Schools

For Clare
without whom . . .

A Shared Vision

Education in Church Schools

David W. Lankshear

National Society/Church House Publishing
Church House, Great Smith Street, London SW1P 3NZ

ISBN 0 7151 4815 X

First published in 1992 by The National Society
and Church House Publishing

Cover photographs by Keith Ellis and David W. Lankshear

Cover design by Bill Bruce at *The Creative House*

Typeset by *The Creative House*

Printed in England by Rapier Press

Contents

Preface

The parents were gathering as usual outside the school gate. While waiting for their children to come out of school they watched a workman erecting a new school notice board. It had been some years since the old one had blown down in a gale and a few years before that since anyone had been able to read the faded writing on it. In bright new lettering the notice said:

St Agatha's Church of England Primary School

"Here", said one of the parents turning to her neighbour, "What does it mean *Church of England Primary School*?".
"Dunno", said her friend. "Maybe it's something to do with the Vicar being in the school a lot. They say he's always here at coffee time."

Of course Church schools are about being much more than schools where the local vicar is a welcome visitor, nor are they the only ones where parish clergy are greeted with a smile and a cup of coffee. Anglican schools have a long and proud history of service within the developing education system of this country. As reforms are introduced to meet changing needs it is important that the teachers, governors, parents and church members take the time to discuss and renew their understanding of the place of the Church school in their community.

In England and Wales there are nearly 21,000 primary schools; of these just under 5,000 are Anglican primary schools, all of which have been founded by the Church through the action of individuals, parishes and dioceses often acting together and with the National Society. This book is about education in those schools.

As the new arrangements for school management, the content of the school curriculum, the appraisal of teachers and the

9

inspection of schools are being introduced, it seems appropriate to bring together a range of ideas about the way in which Anglican Church schools can operate.

This book is drawn from my experience as a headteacher of a Church primary school and as a member of two diocesan education teams. In this latter capacity I have visited many Church schools in recent years. I have also led training activities for governors, headteachers and teachers in them. The ideas contained in the pages that follow have been refined through this process and I am grateful to all those who have helped to develop them, particularly those who have asked the difficult and challenging questions as so often they have been the catalyst in the process. All the anecdotes contained within the book are true, and are drawn from my own experience or that of close colleagues.

I have not attempted to make this an academic book in that I have not sought to root all the arguments in the literature of the philosophy and theology of education. Rather it is intended to stimulate thought, discussion and action both with reference to the areas that are covered within its pages, and with reference to those that are perceived as having been omitted.

The book is addressed principally to teachers, but I hope that it may also be of interest to clergy, governors, parents, students and others interested in the quality of education in Church schools. For many the contents of some chapters will be familiar, and so in order to enable readers to skim those topics on which they are expert I have made extensive use of sub-headings in the text. Each chapter ends with two or three questions designed to stimulate reflection and discussion.

Every Anglican Church school is different and it is not possible to write a prescription that will immediately provide a panacea for all the real or perceived needs of the individual classroom or school. What I hope to achieve is a challenge to stimulate all Anglican promary schools to think through their practice in the light of their Christian foundation, and the changes that have recently been required of them. The result should be that they develop a renewed vision of Christian service to the Church and the wider community through the provision of high quality education for the children.

I must express my thanks to Helen Woodroffe, Leslie Francis, Geoffrey Duncan, Alan Brown and Christopher Herbert, who all read the first draft of this book and made so many constructive comments on it. Without their assistance it would have been much worse than it is. I must also thank the National Society's Book Editor, Alan Mitchell, for his patience and careful work in correcting the text. In doing this he joins the group of people who understand some of the reasons for my failings as a teacher of English recounted in the last anecdote in the book.

David W. Lankshear
December 1991

1

What is a Church School?

The differences between a Church school and a county school

> I was talking to a very experienced headteacher who had just taken up a new post as head of a Church school. It was early in the September term. She said, "Do you know, on the day before term started three parents came into school to tell me that their marriages had broken up during the holidays, and about the resultant changes in their circumstances. In my previous school this would have been usual, but somehow in a Church school I thought it would be different."

Many people working in education think that "somehow in a church school it would be different" and are then surprised to find that the difference is not where they expect it to be. Anglican schools that are part of the maintained system serve local communities, and so tend to reflect life as it is experienced in such places. If there are pressures on marriage, these will be felt by the parents of children in Church schools as well as the parents of children in county schools. If there are events that disturb or enliven the community, their effects will be experienced in Church schools as well as county schools. Parents may be kind and caring in both Church and county schools. Identifying the differences that make or should make Church schools distinct becomes more complex the more you examine the problem. Should you look for differences in the school management, the curriculum, the ethos, the children who attend, the staff or even the buildings? Perhaps there is no difference between Anglican schools and county schools.

These difficulties of definition are what create the classic interview question.

> "Now, tell me Miss Smith, what do you think is the difference between a Church school and a county school?"
> "Er, well, um, Church schools are more caring, and, er, well, it's about sharing and trying to be good."
> "I see, you don't think that makes the Church sound rather like the Co-op? No, no need to answer that, thank you Miss Smith."

Poor Miss Smith. Another victim of a bored interviewer. Perhaps she should have had the courage to turn the tables and ask her persecutors for their ideas on the subject. This would be almost certain to produce some embarrassed shuffling of feet amongst members of the interviewing panel. Too often it seems that no-one is able to provide a satisfactory answer to this deceptively simple question.

In his book *Partnership in Rural Education*[1] Leslie Francis drew attention to these problems by producing research evidence which showed that not only was there lack of understanding amongst teachers of the role of a Church school, but also some teachers did not even know that they were teaching in one. Since the publication of that study, new Education Acts and the development of schemes of teacher appraisal and school evaluation have all increased the need for teachers, governors and the Church in general to think again and with clarity about what it means to teach in a Church school.

The factual background

There are 4903 Anglican primary schools in England and Wales, providing education for approximately 680,000 children between the ages of four and eleven (DES Statistical Summary 1991).[2] There are also 225 Anglican secondary schools, although the distribution of these does not represent the equivalent range of coverage offered by Anglican primary schools. In each case these figures include some middle schools. There are 72 Anglican middle schools which are deemed to be primary, and 69 that are deemed to be secondary). The Roman Catholic Church has a large number of Church schools with a better balance between primary and secondary schools. Some other Christian denominations also have schools in the maintained sector as does the Jewish community. Recently there have been a number of requests from private Muslim and non-denominational Christian schools for aided status, but so far these have not obtained the necessary approvals.

Many Church schools were founded in the nineteenth century and are often to be found in the centres of population that existed then. Thus there are many Church of England primary schools in villages, and in the long established inner city areas but few in the more recently developed suburbs. As a result of this historic distribution and the way in which the areas that they serve have changed, Anglican schools can seem to be very different from each other. In 1811 the National Society was founded to support the development of Anglican schools. Today it continues to work actively in this field as a Church voluntary body and has particular responsibilities for the promotion of Religious Education.

As it was not until 1870 that there was a means whereby schools could be founded other than by voluntary action there was a long period when the only education available to the young was that provided through the Church of England and other churches or groups with a similar commitment to education. Indeed the Forster Act of 1870 only created the possibility of the gaps in the Church's provision being filled. There have been many changes in the way in which the education service of this country has been organised since the 1870 Act, but Church of England schools have continued to play a major role in the system.

Different types of Church school

The 1944 Education Act provided the framework for the present way in which the Church is involved in schools by creating two broad types of Church school, the aided and the controlled.

In Aided schools:
1. The school is owned by trustees, as part of a Church educational trust.
2. The foundation (church) governors are in the majority on the governing body.
3. The staff are employed by the governors.
4. The governors are responsible for external maintenance of the building, with the exception of the school kitchen areas, and for funding improvements to it. For this they receive a grant (currently 85%) from the Department of Education and Science or the Welsh Office for approved projects.
5. Religious Education is taught in accordance with the provisions of the Trust Deed, unless parents request teaching in accordance with the Agreed Syllabus and there is no other convenient school which the children can attend where this is offered.
6. Worship is conducted according to the provisions of the Trust Deed.
7. The governors are responsible for the admissions to the school.

In Controlled schools:
1. The school is owned by trustees, as part of a Church educational trust.
2. The foundation (church) governors are in a minority on the governing body.
3. The staff are employed by the local authority.
4. The local authority is responsible for the external maintenance of the building and for funding improvements to

it, although the authority may delegate most of its responsibilities to the governing body.

5. Religious Education is taught in accordance with the local authority's Agreed Syllabus, although religious education in accordance with the trust deed may be provided if parents request it for their children.

6. Worship is conducted according to the provisions of the Trust Deed.

7. The local authority is responsible for the admissions to the school.

These are the broad areas of difference, although some others will emerge in the course of the book. In some places there are Special Agreement schools, which share most of the characteristics of aided status except that the local authority is the employer of the staff. There are, of course local variations on these basic provisions, mostly as a result of the way in which a particular school was founded.

It may come as a surprise to some to realise that when they read the words Church of England (Controlled) School on a school notice board, it does not mean that it is a school "controlled" by the Church of England. In fact it means that this is a school in which the formal powers of the Church are less than in a Church of England (Aided) school. However this should not be taken to indicate that the Church is less concerned about them or less committed to promoting good education within them. While the legal framework leads to a wide range of differences in practice, so too do the communities in which Church schools are placed. At one level there may seem to be little in common between a three class village school in the Lake District, a twenty class school in a London suburb, and a seven class school in an inner city, except the words "Church of England" on the school's name board. However all should share the commitment, support and interest of the Church in the work that they are doing.

The debate about Church schools

Today, as in the past, there are differing views about Church schools. There are those who would argue that the schools are provided by the Church and are a major potential asset in the Church's work of evangelism and Christian nurture. This has been explored in books by Leslie Francis and reports like *All God's Children?.*[3] Evidence from the *Children, Young People and the Church* project has demonstrated the positive impact on parish life of the presence of a Church school in the parish. Others have argued that the Church offers partnership in the state education system as part of its witness to Christ, and the key role of the Church school is to be a good school run within the context of a Christian community. This was explored in *The Fourth R: The Durham Report on Religious Education,*[4] *A Future in Partnership*[5] and previous Church reports. Those opposed to the existence of Church schools see them as anachronistic and socially divisive, and would wish to see further development of Church schools inhibited or even all Church schools absorbed in the county school sector. These arguments have been advanced in publications from the Socialist Education Association, the Commission for Racial Equality and the partners in mission report *To a Rebellious House.*[6]

The relevance of the debate

These debates about the Church's continuing involvement in the provision of schools inevitably have political and financial dimensions, and many of us would wish to make a contribution to that discussion. However, regardless of the view that is taken of these schools the fact remains that they exist. This implies that we must reinforce their continued existence, take seriously what is happening within them and seek to ensure that the experience of education that we offer the children enables them to learn as effectively as possible. This can only be achieved if the governors, teachers, parents and church come together in a shared commitment to enhance that educational experience.

In recent years much has happened to alter the structures of our education system. New management systems have been introduced which, in some respects, have blurred the difference between aided schools and others, by giving county and controlled schools more independence. The National Curriculum and its accompanying assessments have increased the central co-ordination of the curriculum. New procedures are being developed for teacher appraisal and school inspection. In all of this it has been easy to forget that the purposes of schools are principally achieved in the education which they offer to children, and not in who governs them, how they are administered or the accuracy with which the legal framework, within which they function, is drafted. These things are important, but they are not of first importance. In the beginning was the child.

Questions for reflection and discussion

1. What differences are observable in your local community between Anglican and county schools?
2. Is there a local debate about the place of Church schools? What views are being expressed?

2

The Children Who Come

An introduction to admissions policies

Matthew was four and a bit when I met him in the reception class of a Church of England primary school. He was painting a picture, the paint brush held tightly in his fist. In the centre of the paper was a large green, blue, red, yellow and brown blob. I got down beside him, and looked carefully at the picture. "Now, let me see," I said, "I think that you have painted a picture of a hippopotamus." "You're right," he said.

Matthew is much like any other child beginning school, finding his way in a new environment and exploring a variety of new experiences, not least humouring unknown visitors. However as he is in a Church school, it is worth reflecting how he came to be there. Some people will assume that, because he is at a Church of England school, his parents must be active members of the Church of England. Others will assume that he is at the school, because it is the nearest one to his home, or because his parents decided that it would be the best school for him to attend. All these could be good reasons for Matthew to be at his particular school. All of them might be true.

Aided school admissions policies

Admissions to Church of England Aided schools are the responsibility of the governing body, who must produce and publish an admissions policy for the school. This policy will establish how decisions are made if the school is oversubscribed. If there are fewer children whose parents wish them to come to the school than the school has places for, then all the children seeking admission will be admitted.

In some Aided schools the admissions policy might look like this:

Admissions Policy for St Agatha's Church of England Aided Primary School, Somewhere Hill, London.
Where the number of applications exceeds the number of places available the governors will have regard to the following criteria:
1. whether the parents are involved in the work and worship of St Agatha's Church;
2. whether the child already has a brother or sister attending the school who will still be at the school when the child is admitted;
3. whether the parents are involved in the work and worship of another Christian church in the deanery of Somewhere Hill, for which St Agatha's is the nearest Church school;
4. whether the parents wish their child to attend a Church school.
Within these four criteria the governors will take account of any special medical, social or educational needs, for which evidence can be produced, which would suggest that the child would benefit from admission to the school. In the case of these criteria not being sufficient, the governors will also have regard to the distance that the child would have to travel to this school.

The impact of such a policy over the years would be to ensure that the children who came to the school were largely those who were being brought up within the Christian faith community. It would also ensure that children with special needs had some measure of priority for admission, and that no child travelled an unacceptable distance to reach the school.

Alternatively an admissions policy could look like this:

Admissions policy for St Freda's Church of England Aided Primary School, Little Puddling in the Marsh, Mummersetshire. Where the number of applications exceeds the number of places that are available the governors will have regard to the following criteria:
1. whether the child is resident in the ecclesiastical parish of Little Puddling in the Marsh;
2. whether the child has a brother or sister attending the school, who will still be attending the school when the child is admitted;
3. whether the child is resident in that part of Greater Puddling which is east of the old railway line;
4. whether the child is resident in that part of Nether Puddling north of a line drawn along the centre of Church Lane from the railway line to Marsh farm and then along the west bank of Parsons Brook to the C1000 road;
5. whether the parents not being resident in the above area are involved in the work and worship of a church in the Under Marsh group of parishes;
6. the distance that the child would have to travel to school.

Such a policy would ensure that the school served the village in which it was set and the surrounding community, and would depend, for its validity, on the extent to which it represented the conditions in the Trust Deed created when the school was founded or subsequent emendations to it.

No-one should underestimate the problems faced by governing bodies in administering these policies. They can cause much heart searching. Even when governors have been asked to work through a training exercise on admissions using mythical children and a non-existent school, people have said "I don't like doing this." If it is hard in fiction, how much more difficult is it when the real decision has to be made between two children, when governors would really like to admit them both. The 1980 Education Act required that this process should be brought into the open for the first time and ensured that parents had the right of appeal against the decisions of governors. Although this has been important in establishing open government in this aspect of the management of schools, it has also caused more people to become involved in wrestling with the decisions and worrying about the problems they cause.

You will find neither St Agatha's nor St Freda's on any map, but in their different ways both of these schools are set within the Anglican tradition of providing education. St Agatha's follows the principle of a Church school education for the children of church parents, St Freda's the principle of offering a service to the local community by educating the children of the community. Most Church of England Aided schools would identify with one of these two principles and some would see themselves as embracing both. If you want to see where a school that you know stands on this, you will need to look at its admissions policy.

Controlled school admissions policies

Admissions in a controlled school are a matter for the local authority. They must publish the policy, but they also have a duty to consult with the governors of the school. The only way in which a geographical boundary can be used to establish an admissions policies is if it is a reflection of the Trust Deed of the school. Therefore it can be quite difficult for an authority to draw up a policy that enables it to make fair decisions about admissions. A typical controlled school admissions policy could look like this:

Admissions policy for St Marcion's Church of England Controlled Primary School.

If the number of applicants exceeds the number of places available the authority will have regard to the following criteria:

1. whether the child has a brother or sister attending the school, who will still be attending the school when the child is admitted;

2. whether the child is resident in the ecclesiastical parish of St Marcion's under the Railway;

3. whether the parents of the child are involved in the work and worship of St Marcion's Church (NB not more than four places will be allocated on this criterion in each year. Decisions on admissions in this category will only be made after consultation with the foundation governors of the school);

4. whether the parents wish their child to attend the school.

The authority will have regard to the fact that St Marcion's is the designated school for the physically handicapped in the Railway Ward of Somewhereville, and also the distance that the child would have to travel to this school.

This policy contains two special features, which will not appear in every case. Firstly it contains a limited concession to the Church foundation, which would enable the governors to admit up to four children of church parents who live outside the parish, provided that the school has met its commitments to brothers and sisters of existing pupils and children living in the parish. It is sometimes in the authority's interest to make this concession as it is then able to argue that there is no liability on it to provide a contribution to the travelling costs of such children to an aided school. Secondly it makes mention of specific educational needs for which the school has been equipped. In this case it may be that it is the only primary school in one area of the town which has been adapted to be used by children in wheelchairs. Clearly it is a good use of resources to ensure that those children who need this facility and who apply for a place at the school are admitted.

Parental assumptions

There have been no scientific studies of the reasons why parents choose to send their children to Church schools. However there is much discussion and supposition about their reasons both in the Church and the teaching profession. The opponents of Church schools suggest that most of the reasons are based on prejudice and the wish of parents to protect their children from the influence of the real world. Some even suggest that there exists a racist element in this. Within the Church there are sometimes doubts expressed about the extent to which the church allegiances claimed stand up to scrutiny, in particular the inclusion of a requirement in an admissions policy that a child be baptised is said to lead to an increase in requests for baptism from parents who rarely if ever attend church. Against this it is argued that there are many parents who value the fact that within Church schools matters of religion are taken seriously, who perceive that there is an ordered learning environment in Church schools or who wish to be able to choose the school which seems most likely to meet the needs of their child. These are seen by many as valid reasons for parents choosing a Church school. Many such parents will be in that group in the population that consider themselves to be Christian, while not at the present attending a Christian place of worship.

The admission policies shown above will have differing results on the likelihood of parents obtaining access to Church schools for their children. St Agatha's will tend to produce a majority of parents with a strong commitment to the school as a Church school. The other two policies will produce parents who have a commitment to the school as a neighbourhood school, but perhaps with less concern about its Church foundation.

The implications for the school

Clearly the admissions policy will determine some of the assumptions that can be made about the children who come to the school. In St Agatha's it might be reasonable to assume that the children will all have had some experience of attending a church or other place of worship. Some may be very regular in their attendance. A few may find that as they grow up they need the opportunity to reflect on their experience of church in a context that does not involve their parents, so that they can come to their own decisions about the faith in which their parents are nurturing them. In such a school it might be quite usual to find regular celebrations of the Eucharist if the worship at St Agatha's is eucharistically based. Even if this is not the case, there will certainly be carefully planned links between the worship in school and the worship in church. It might also be assumed that a number of the parents will be very supportive of the school's programme of Religious Education. However, it could not be assumed that, because the parents are involved in Church life, they are immune from the problems and temptations of the world. At the beginning of the first chapter I quoted an incident in which a headteacher quickly found how wrong such an assumption could be. Nor should it be assumed that such a school will be full of children from white middle-class homes as there will be children from all ethnic groups whose parents are active members of the Church of England or another Christian Church. Such children would be admitted to Church schools even where the policy is overtly church orientated as at St Agatha's. Indeed, for historical reasons, the spread of Church of England schools is probably thinnest in the suburbs of the big cities, where middle-class families are most often expected to be living.

The assumptions that can be made about children in schools like St Freda's or St Marcion's are rather different. They would only be the assumptions that you could make about the children in the village as a whole. These might vary considerably, depending on the nature of the village. Indeed in the specific example given, the assumptions made about the children from Little Puddling might be quite different from the assumptions made about those in Great Puddling or Nether Puddling.

Perhaps it is dangerous to make assumptions at all. Once the children are in school it will be the task of the staff to come to know them as individuals, not as typical residents of Little Puddling or typical sons and daughters of the worshippers at St Agatha's church.

Some of the children who come to the school will have special educational needs. Indeed the policy for St Agatha's specifically provides for such children to have some priority within each of its categories. This reflects a commitment to the education of these children which both governors and teachers will need to take seriously.

Opponents of Church schools often suggest that the schools seek to avoid accepting an appropriate proportion of these children. There is little foundation for such an accusation as there is usually either a commitment to all the children of a geographical area or a specific commitment such as the one mentioned above. Therefore no teacher should be under the misapprehension that they are less likely to benefit from having such children in their class if they teach in a Church school.

Children no less than adults are made in the image of God. As such they can reflect God to us if only we can allow that to be a possibility. We have to base our approach to the children on this assumption which is rooted in the creation story in Genesis and our Lord's commandment to love one another. If we do this then the need for assumptions about how they will behave, what will interest them or develop their experience will be set in a proper context.

Questions for reflection and discussion

1. What is the basis for admission in the Church schools in our area?
2. What assumptions are made about the children who attend them?
3. How should acknowledging that children are made in the image of God affect the way that they are treated in school?

3

The Curriculum

The existence of a Christian view of the school curriculum

The year six class was taking a standardised test of reading comprehension under examination conditions as part of the LEA's monitoring of standards. Five minutes into the test a boy stood up and began to walk across the room.

"David, where are you going?"

"There is a word in this piece that I don't understand, so I am going to look it up in the dictionary."

As the teacher told him to return to his place and continue the test without the aid of the dictionary, he was left to reflect that, while David might not get the marks in the test, he had revealed that what had been taught by the school had been absorbed. It was the test that was alien to the school's practice and to life.

On the opening page of the *Education Reform Act 1988* the basic curriculum philosophy which underpins it is spelt out. It states:

The curriculum for a maintained school satisfies the requirements of this section if it is a balanced and broadly based curriculum which

(a) promotes the spiritual, moral, cultural, mental and physical development of pupils at the school and of society; and

(b) prepares such pupils for the opportunities, responsibilities and experiences of adult life.

Given this basic statement which applies to Church of England schools as to all others in the maintained system, does the context of a Church of England school affect the way that we approach the teaching of the subjects other than Religious Education that come within the school's curriculum plan? If so, how does it affect them? Is there a Christian view of mathematics or science?

At one level it has been argued that this is not so. Professor Paul Hirst went so far as to argue that Christian belief and educational principles are logically incompatible.[1] Others have questioned the ability of a Christian school to deliver a multi-cultural education.[2] However the Church of England has shown itself to be sensitive to these issues, and has sought to develop an approach to the curriculum which is true to the gospel and sensitive to the beliefs of others. A booklet published by the National Society in 1990 entitled *The Curriculum: A Christian View* continues this tradition which has its roots in the report *The Fourth R* published in 1970. The point to be remembered here is that all teaching is value laden. It is not possible to be neutral. Therefore it is more honest to be open with both parents and pupils about the stance that is being taken, than to claim a level of objectivity that cannot be achieved in practice.

There are a number of concerns which Christians have, or share with others, that the Church might reasonably expect to find reflected in the work of its schools. To illustrate this I have chosen a selection of such concerns and worked out some thoughts about how each of them might be applied to one area of the National Curriculum. It is not an exhaustive list, nor is this approach meant to suggest that the topic only applies to this area of the curriculum. These are illustrations only.

Values in literature

The staff meeting was proceeding quietly in a room overlooking the road down which many of the children walked home from school.

Suddenly the headteacher's announcements of the arrangements for sports day was interrupted by a shout.

"Look at that!"

We looked. One of the year five boys, well known for his prowess at sport and not well known for his commitment to his lessons, was walking down the road with his eyes glued to the book that he was reading.

"I never thought that I would see the day," said his teacher. Deeply satisfied the staff returned once more to the arrangements for the first year three-legged race. It will come as no surprise to learn that the boy was reading one of the *Narnia* books.

Immediately on seeing the title of this section you may be assuming that the suggestion is that the books on each classroom shelf should be subjected to some kind of censorship. This is not so. The starting point is that every teacher makes choices about the books that the children will read every day. This is done partly by what is selected to be put on the shelf, and also by which of those books have attention drawn to them during the course of the class's work. The English Working Party of the National Curriculum Council drew up some of the criteria that teachers could use in this selection. They mentioned the quality of the illustrations, the quality of the writing, and the print amongst other things. Teachers will recognise these as issues with which they are familiar. We try to ensure that our children see good quality books in terms of their production. However the same working party was hesitant to suggest issues to do with the content of the books, and yet teachers make judgements based on the content of a book every day. For example, "this book is appropriate to children aged eight years old or over" is a sentence common to the reviews that teachers write, and no-one would suggest that five-year-olds should be reading sexually explicit novels. The issue is then the criteria that teachers use to make judgements about the books that will be available for their children to read.

All authors build into their books two assumptions. The first is about the readers. Who are they? What will they bring to reading this book? What may they take from it? The second assumption is about the way in which the world works. This is most easily perceived in works of fantasy or science fiction, where new worlds are created, but is also very evident in works that assume that "no girl is complete without her pony" or "all boys are interested in sport".

It cannot be right for teachers to decide that only books with a certain "world view" are to be made available to their children. Nor would the situation where a seventeen-year-old is still reading the children's books by Roald Dahl be regarded as satisfactory to teachers committed to ensuring that the pupils in their charge are becoming mature readers. Presumably therefore the objective must be to have a broad range of world views available for the children, growing ever wider as the children mature, and to seek to encourage the children to read across this range as extensively as possible.

Teachers, like the one in the story which began this section, will rejoice at the breakthrough that occurs when children first discover an author or a genre of books which they enjoy, but they will not be satisfied that their task is complete at that point. Good teachers will seek to develop the range of pupils' reading so that gradually the whole breadth of adult literature is opened up to them.

In all teachers there should be a desire to ensure that their children are understanding what they are reading. Sometimes this will be done by asking factual questions about the content, but perhaps more often it will be done by asking the children to reflect on what they have been reading.

Initially it could be that they are asked to continue the story, or write another story using the same characters. As the children mature they may be asked to think about or discuss the actions of the characters, or to consider their feelings or the decisions that they made during the story. At secondary level the assumptions that the author has brought to the book may also be explored. This will reflect the growing maturity of the pupils as readers and the "multi-layered" quality of good literature.

There are those who would wish to argue for the inclusion of some specific world views within the classroom texts or the exclusion of others. Each teacher and school will have their own thoughts on this matter, and these should be discussed so that a coherent policy can emerge, but it is important that the range of literature that the children meet should be at least as broad and probably broader than their own experience of life. Within that range will be books which feature two and one parent families, people for whom religious belief is important and people for whom it is not, the experience of being human in various parts of the world, and books that seek to imagine what it would be like to be human or to share human characteristics in other settings. Every reader of this book will want to further broaden the range of examples.

While much of what has been covered in this section may have been understood to refer to works of fiction, there should be no doubt that the same criteria also apply to other books which are found in the classroom. The range of world views and of assumptions made by the authors about their readers should be as wide in non-fiction as in fiction.

Awe and wonder in mathematics

Owen was not among the brightest boys in the class, but he had been listening to a discussion about manned space flight with growing interest. There was a puzzled look on his face, as he put his hand up to ask a question.

"Yes, Owen?"

"You say that the shuttle is spinning round the earth, and that the earth is also spinning."

"Yes."
"Well if that is true, how do they work out when to fire the rockets that will bring it back to the landing site?"
There was a long pause.

Owen had thought out a problem and presented it in a way which went beyond the knowledge of anyone in the room, including the teacher. The answer had to be something to the effect that clearly the scientists and mathematicians could work it out, because they showed that they had done so every time the shuttle landed. We could also see that this was a difficult problem, because it was beyond us even to work out how to begin to find the answer. Perhaps not very satisfactory as a reply, but Owen was satisfied, at least for the moment.

Seeing beyond what we know, catching a glimpse of possibilities, is certainly one of the starting points of wonder. Perhaps it seems strange to talk about awe and wonder in the context of mathematics, but if it is accepted that mathematics is more than just a useful set of tricks to help you solve problems, then it is possible to suggest that even here the seeds of wonder do exist.

Many teachers will have spent some time with their class enabling them to experience some of the exciting shapes and patterns that can be created using only straight lines. Initially it may be the discovery that enough of them drawn carefully can create something that looks more and more like a curve. Perhaps it may also have involved making more and more complex patterns with two dimensional shapes. If at this point some of the patterns used for the decoration of mosques or the work of such artists as Eischer are introduced to the children then the concept of beauty within, or derived from mathematical ideas, is within their grasp.

Mathematics, like music, is an international language to which many nations and cultures have contributed. Our respect for such contributions is important to any truly multi-cultural approach to the curriculum, and we must be careful not to limit our teaching in this area to only that which we perceive to be useful.

The world of mathematics is one of order, elegance and beauty, as well as excitement. If we leave this out of our teaching we will run the danger of ensuring that future generations find mathematics as boring as the past ones have done. We cannot afford this, nor are we properly reflecting the wonder and beauty of creation and therefore the creator unless we include it within our teaching programme.

Respect for life in science

A group of children were looking at a small field mouse which had been caught in a humane trap by the conservation centre for them to study on their visit. (It was released again that evening back into its own territory.) There was much amused comment as the mouse scampered about his cage. The comment reflected excited but careful observation. A child started to tap the glass side of the cage with his pencil presumably to attract the creature's attention. Another child leaned across and moved the pencil away saying, "Don't do that you'll frighten it." There followed a short discussion about how the mouse would be feeling, and whether it was really frightened. Sadly this promising debate was interrupted when the teacher asked the children to move on from observation to the next stage of their work. Distinctly heard above the general working hum of voices came the comment, "Oh, we haven't got to draw it, have we?"

There is a body of opinion within western cultures that understands the earth, its resources and the life that it supports as an endless source of wealth to be exploited by man. Some Christians take this view, but perhaps they need to read the second chapter of Genesis more carefully. That chapter suggests that we should regard ourselves as stewards of creation, not exploiters of it. Other faith communities may have something to teach us in this area in so far as they make clear their understanding of the inter-relationship that exists between all living things. This is one of many opportunities to include a consideration of what is important to other faiths and groups of people within the curriculum.

As a result of the introduction of the National Curriculum the proportion of curriculum time given over to science in primary schools is growing. Teachers will need to be careful about the understanding that children acquire about the importance of life. It is all too easy, in putting life under the microscope, to divorce ourselves from our responsibility for it. Throughout our work in science we need to ensure that children and young people grow not only in understanding of the way in which the world and those things living on it function, but also in understanding of our responsibility for facilitating that growth. At one level it may mean observing plants as they grow using only ways which do not stop that growth, that is without picking specimens or damaging them unless this is specifically required. At another it may mean only gathering live specimens of animals or insects that we are certain that we can return to their natural habitat. However it should also warn us to be careful about our use of materials, and to seek to use materials as many times as possible before they are disposed of, and then ensuring that their disposal is managed carefully. It would seem perverse to run a topic on recycling without using recycled materials and then making them available for further recycling at the end of the topic.

These are not meant to be a set of minor rules but rather indicators of an approach which seeks to teach by example, so that what is learned is more than what is contained in the objectives for a particular lesson.

Inspiration and motivation in the arts

We were practising "Amazing Grace" and the singing was flat and dull. It would have been possible to stop and go over the notes and the words again in order to improve the standard of the singing. However for some reason I did not do that. Instead I told them the story of John Newton, the writer of the hymn. The idea of a former slave trader now become a Christian and writing the words from personal experience seemed to catch their imagination. The singing improved.

It could be that the singing of the children in the above story improved simply because there had been a break, or change of activity, but I suspect that for some, at least, better understanding led to better performance. The National Curriculum is rightly drawing our attention towards a better balance in our teaching in this broad area of the curriculum, away from concentration on the children's own creativity towards a consideration of other people's creativity as well as their own. This naturally leads to a consideration of the artist, the musician, the sculptor and the performer. As a result there seem then to be two questions that we need to enable our children to consider.

1. What did they do?
Perhaps this is the proper starting point. As the children are brought into contact with works of art, including performance, then it is natural that they should begin to identify certain individuals whose work they enjoy, or which they dislike. This should motivate them to find out more about these individuals, or at least the ones that they like, and the work that they did. Naturally part of the children's education will be to be brought into contact with as wide a range of the arts as possible, and to be helped to experience them in ways that are appropriate. Initially this may include such simple things as learning to listen carefully, or to observe.

2. Why did they do it?
If this question is interpreted at the level of "Why did the artist put a shell in the front of that man's hat?" or "Why are there

only patterns in the decoration of a mosque and no representations of people or things?", it may lead to the beginnings of an understanding of the "vocabulary" of the art in question. This could include a consideration of the way in which symbols are used or the way in which certain disciplines are accepted by some groups of artists. However the more important part of this question deals with the artists' motivation and their sources of ideas and inspiration. This inevitably brings the child or young person towards a consideration of those things which were important to the creative artist. These could be simple ideas such as the nature of colour or the rhythm of the words or notes, or complex ideas such as human love or faith. This exploration of "why" questions may arise from the growth of knowledge about the artist as a human being as well as about their art.

It is as the children begin to understand the nature of the second order questions and to explore some of the answers that are valid for a particular creative artist that they will begin to develop a framework for understanding the arts, and also for coming to terms with their own creativity.

A framework for the curriculum

In this chapter it has not been possible to provide a complete overview of all the areas of the curriculum and all the frameworks which can be applied to them which are drawn from a Christian understanding of the world. All that has been attempted is to provide a few examples. In the following matrix the examples selected are shown in relation to each other. Those areas of the matrix which have been briefly explored are marked ****.

Framework for exploration	School subject areas				
	English	Maths	Science	Arts	Others
Values	* * * *				
Beauty		* * * *			
Respect			* * * *		
Inspiration				* * * *	
Others					

Assessment has not been mentioned in this chapter but of course in any curriculum planning assessment must have its place. However it is important that there is a distinction retained between the form of classroom based assessment used by teachers to monitor work, and the real situation in which children show whether they can apply what they have learned.

From success to failure in a few seconds

Derrick was very proud of his bicycle. It gleamed when he brought it to school for the training that led up to him taking his cycling proficiency test. He worked hard at learning the highway code, harder than he did at most lessons on the timetable. It was no surprise that when the day of the test came, he passed with flying colours, indeed top of the whole group. Derrick could not remember being best at anything before in his life. His teachers immediately began to calculate how they could build on this new success to motivate him to greater efforts in other aspects of his school work.

Derrick felt wonderful as he set off to cycle home after the test. The school was in a quiet cul-de-sac, at the end of which was a fairly busy main road. So proud was Derrick of passing his cycling proficiency, that he quite forgot to stop at the end of the lane and check the traffic. He cycled straight out into the main road.

Fortunately the car that hit him was going quite slowly. Derrick was off school for two days and then came back with his arm in a sling, a simple break that healed quickly and completely. The bicycle however was never quite the same again.

No experience is ever wasted. This story became a cautionary tale told to every subsequent group of cycling proficiency testees before they set of for home after their tests. None of them ever had an accident.

Questions for reflection and discussion

1. What would you include as examples to illustrate the areas of the matrix which have not been considered in this chapter?
2. Which other subject areas and frameworks for exploring them would you wish to add to the matrix?

4

Religious Education

In a lesson with year three children a teacher had told one of the
parables of Jesus. She went on to explain its meaning. Within her
explanation the parable meant "behave yourself in the playground".
Not everyone is aware that our Lord told a story with this meaning,
so a moment of reflection may be necessary before it is identified.

The story was the parable of the wise man building his house on the
rock. In the teacher's explanation this meant, build your life on firm
foundations, which means obey the rules, which means behave
yourself in the playground.

Teachers who work in Church schools must accept that there will
be an expectation that the Religious Education in the school and in
each classroom will be of the highest possible quality. Therefore the
subject needs to be considered in some depth in this book, despite
the fact that it is also considered in other publications by the
National Society and by local dioceses.

The legal framework

The first important thing to understand in approaching Religious
Education is that it is a serious academic subject, just like any other
subject on the school curriculum. It is also part of every child's
entitlement within the curriculum as it is a legal requirement. It was
first made so in the 1944 Education Act. The 1988 Education
Reform Act re-affirmed this by identifying Religious Education and
the National Curriculum as together forming the Basic Curriculum
which must be taught to every child in all maintained schools.

The only exception to these provisions occurs when the parents of a particular child decide to exercise their right to withdraw their child from this subject on grounds of conscience. The parents must inform the school of their decision in writing, and only then will the child be excluded from the subject. At present only a very small percentage of parents exercise this right. Therefore, for the vast majority of children, the school has a responsibility to provide a properly organised, well constructed, interesting programme of Religious Education.

Such a programme should include consideration of the faith communities in this country, what they do and why they do it, and also the opportunity for the children to reflect on their own experience as this develops in the light of what they know about the faith in which they are growing up, even if this is secular materialism or a belief in the God of the Christmas card and the requirement to be good to your neighbours.

In Controlled Schools the Agreed Syllabus, appropriate for the Local Education Authority in which the school is located, will usually set the framework for the subject, unless the parents specifically request that "denominational teaching" be made available. The Education Reform Act 1988 requires that Agreed Syllabuses for Religious Education "shall reflect the fact that the religious traditions in Great Britain are in the main Christian". These provisions will apply to all Church schools where the Religious Education is conducted in accordance with an Agreed Syllabus, which will include Grant Maintained schools that were previously Controlled schools, and Aided or Special Agreement schools where the parents have requested "Agreed Syllabus" Religious Education. In Aided or Special Agreement schools the legal requirement is that Religious Education should be taught in accordance with the provisions of the school's Trust Deed, unless the parents have asked for teaching in accordance with the Agreed Syllabus. The Diocesan Syllabus will normally provide the framework for teaching in accordance with the Trust Deed. The basis for this being that the Diocesan Bishop is understood to be the final judge of what the Trust Deed requirements mean in practice, and, as the Diocesan Syllabus is published with his authority, it provides an indication of how he would interpret the provisions of the deed in a particular school. Grant Maintained schools that were previously Aided should also be following the Diocesan Syllabus for the same reasons. Most Church schools will wish to have copies of both the Agreed and Diocesan Syllabuses available in the school so that they have the widest possible range of locally produced resources available for the subject. In almost all Church schools the principal religion to be studied will be Christianity, the only possible exceptions being those where the majority of the children are from another faith community. Even in such schools the requirements of the appropriate syllabus must be met, although sensitivity will be needed for the position of the children from other faiths present in the classroom.

An approach to teaching about Christianity

The Church should be able to assume that the teaching about Christianity will be at its best in Church schools. In part this will be because the Church school should have ready access to the church community and therefore will be able to provide easy contact with that community to be the starting point for work by the children. When we begin to teach any subject with young children we seek a starting point in their own experience, and if this is not available we then seek to provide experience which will serve our educational purpose. The contact that exists between a Church school and its parish should provide this naturally.

If we start from the Christian community, then we shall be in the best position to avoid the trap of confusing religion with culture. It is the experience and practices of the Christian community that will be our safest guide through our teaching about Christianity. What do the people in the Church believe, how does this achieve expression in worship, personal devotion and action? This leads us logically into work on the Bible as the book that Christians use in their worship, private prayer and study, because of its unique place for them in their faith. Approached in this way it also preserves us from the snare of thinking that the Bible is only a book of stories.

Christian worship is the activity of the community of Christians meeting day by day and week by week. It contains patterns in terms of what people do, and in many Churches these follow set forms. In the Church of England these are contained in the Book of Common Prayer and the Alternative Service Book. Both books not only contain the structure of services to be used daily and weekly, but also material for festive and special occasions, which include the rites of passage such as baptism and confirmation. Within these books will be found much of the liturgical material which is part of the common heritage of all Christians. Children may be introduced to these services by visiting churches when they are happening or by seeing video recordings of them.

Many Christians include as part of their response to God a pattern of personal devotion and study. This may include a time of prayer and/or bible reading, perhaps daily or weekly. They may read one or more of the services for themselves. They may read books or guidance notes designed to enhance and develop their understanding of the Bible. They may have patterns of family devotion, which could include saying grace before meals or meeting for Bible study or hymn singing. However not all groups will be family based. Many groups of Christians meet for prayer and Bible study throughout the year and many more make a point of meeting during Lent each year. The children may need some assistance in perceiving this activity, but careful examination of parish magazines and church notice boards and bookstalls will provide evidence for this, as will talking to active members of the Christian community.

Individual Christians' personal faith may well lead them to take actions which other people, particularly those who follow the secularist materialist approach to life, would find extraordinary, in that they do not seem to make sense in the context of an understanding of the world based on the principle of the accumulation of personal wealth as a major pre-occupation. This is not just a matter of those people whose unique devotion to Christ leads them to journey abroad or to take great personal risks with their health or their life to serve Christ by serving mankind. It is also the way in which ordinary everyday Christians give their time, their talents and their money to serve others. The Church's support for charities both home and overseas, its willingness to find time and space for youth work, social work or work among the poor and the dispossessed are all evidence of this, and that evidence can be seen on the notice boards of churches throughout the country week in and week out. Children need to come to an understanding that for people of faith their faith makes a difference. This is why the stories of the heroes of the faith from previous generations are also so important within the Religious Education programme. These also create a link between biblical times and the present, the lack of which so often limits children's understanding of Christianity.

The inclusion of Bible stories in teaching about Christianity

So far there has been reference to the way in which Christians use their Bible but there has been no discussion about the way in which stories from the Bible are selected for classroom use. Therefore it is time that the position of the Bible within the programme of Religious Education teaching was explored. The Bible is made up of many books, some of which include story. Others are books of poetry, law, letters and much more. The books were written over a considerable period of history, and brought together in the form that we have them because generations have found them helpful in their religious life and many believe them to be works inspired by God. They were not written in English. It is important for children to realise this fact, which is obvious to us, because to fail to understand that the Bible used in schools is a translation may lead to all sorts of confusion.

At a suitable point in their school career children will need to undertake work which covers the ground contained in the last paragraph, but before that they will already have become familiar with some of the content of the Bible through their teacher's and parents' story telling. A proportion of them will also have met with the Bible through Church and Sunday school. If you tell stories you have planted a seed in the minds of your listeners, which may grow and develop or which may never germinate. The seed is the experience of life contained within the story you have told. For it to germinate the hearers must reflect on it in the light of their own experience. This will lead them to interpret the story in ways which may be quite different from the way in which the teller of the story intended, and also in ways which may vary with time.

As a consequence of this we must expect that the way in which children understand a story at the moment that we tell it to them will be different from the way in which the adults, that those children will subsequently become, will understand it later in their lives. Left free to make their own response, children may not focus on the story in the way in which we would wish, but may provide us with new insights. Re-hearing the story later may lead to further reflection and different understandings. For this reason it is important to be cautious about providing explanations of stories, as these may curtail the reflective process.

A colleague was telling the story of the Good Samaritan to a group of year six pupils. At the end of the story he asked, "Who was the most important character in the story?" "The innkeeper," said one child. "Why?" "Well, would you trust someone who turned up at your door with a badly beaten man, and said to you here is a fiver, look after this man and if you spend more I will repay you when I am next passing?" "No," said another child, "I thought that it was the donkey." "Why," said the teacher, beginning to feel that this was getting out of hand. "No-one asked the donkey if it wanted to carry the extra weight of the man who had been beaten, but without it the Samaritan would never have got him to the inn."

Naturally we will want the children to focus on our understanding of the story, although both the children in the account above had a point, but we must beware of excluding other interpretations. For me that is one of the lessons to be learned from the story at the beginning of this chapter.

The next issue to be addressed is which Bible stories to include in our Religious Education programme. We cannot tell them all, and not all would be suitable for young children. We have to make a selection. One sound basis for selection is to start from the Christian community. What stories are most important to them? For most Christians the focus of the Bible is given by the story of the death and resurrection of Jesus. Everything else, however important, is secondary to this, and is to be understood in this context. Once that has been accepted as the starting point, then a priority for the other stories begins to emerge. They become more important to teach as they shed light on that one story, and less important as they are further removed from it. You cannot have the death of Jesus without his birth; you cannot know why his death was important without some knowledge of the story of his life told to reveal who he was; and you cannot understand these stories unless you have some knowledge of the Jewish context of his ministry, which provides a focus for selection from the Old Testament. This approach seems to carry the seeds of future learning more effectively than selecting stories on bases such as

a. there are children mentioned in them
b. one of the key words in the story is the same as the title of our current topic
c. someone once wrote a good musical based on this story.

Taking those that are of key importance to Christians as the starting point for the selection of Bible stories for inclusion in the curriculum is important in presenting to the children the faith that is held by the worshipping community. In this way teaching about Christianity can be done with integrity even by those who may have doubts about what they believe themselves, or may be members of another faith. It would be possible for a similar approach to be taken if there was a programme of teaching about Judaism. Which stories are important to the Jews? Why are they important to them?

Teaching about other faiths

Children in Church schools will, at suitable points in their school career, be learning about faiths other than Christianity. This is required of all schools that are using an Agreed Syllabus, and also of most schools that are following diocesan syllabuses. It is important to realise that this is not a study of comparative religion, which is a sophisticated academic exercise, but rather an opportunity for the children to learn something about those things which their neighbours hold to be most important. Of course, in some schools the children have no direct experience of neighbours from other faith communities, nevertheless we are not educating our children only for life within the geographical location in which they are presently living. We must ensure that children grow up understanding that the religious beliefs of others are to be treated sensitively and with respect, wherever they are met, in the next house, the next street or town, on holiday or at work. This is part of the contribution which Religious Education can make to the development of positive relationships between different groups in society.

The approach to Christianity outlined in the main part of this chapter can easily be adapted to form an approach to other world faiths. Where there is access to a local faith community the children can explore what the people within the community do, why they do it and what they believe. They can come to see how their practices relate to their beliefs and the story of their faith. As they develop they will be able to undertake similar explorations of faith communities who are not in the immediate area, particularly if the use of good quality video tapes and well planned visits are included in the programme. This approach does not have to lead to multi-faith syncretism but can honour the distinctiveness of each faith community. Lasting harmony between the faith communities depends on individuals having a clear understanding of their own faith and a respect for the faith of their neighbours.

The place of Moral Education

Thus far this chapter has focused on the content of the Religious Education programme in respect of knowledge about Christianity and other faiths, but that is not all that should be expected of a good quality syllabus. There will need to be a clear understanding of how the syllabus contributes to the development of positive attitudes amongst the children and young people, and also how it contributes to their moral education. Among the ways in which children come to understand what is "good" or "bad" is what they are taught about the choices that other people have had to make, and the basis on which they have made them. Clearly Religious Education has a contribution to make to this process. There can be an examination of the teachings of the different faiths about issues of right or wrong and how believers should make their choices.

Those who would argue that Religious Education should accept the full burden of teaching the children to behave in a moral way will not find this satisfactory. This approach implies that other subjects may also have a contribution to make to the process as will the atmosphere and ethos of the school and the community in which the children live. This is seen by those who wish Religious Education to take the whole responsibility for Moral Education as over complicated, but it is not possible to approach a consideration of the rules by which individuals choose to live in any other way.

The rules and guidance for the conduct of believers within a faith are designed for those believers. Christians follow the teachings of Christ because they believe in him. They accept his commandment to "Love your neighbour as yourself" and identify as heroes of the faith those who have most nearly approached this counsel of perfection. Some Christians will also identify the Ten Commandments as providing further helpful guidance, and, of course Jews will base their teaching on these and the whole of the part of the Bible known as the Torah. These are difficult teachings to follow, because they are a great challenge to adults, let alone children. Believers will attempt to follow them as part of their faith, but that can hardly be expected of non-believers. For others the basis on which they make their moral judgements will depend more on the teaching that they have received from their parents and from school. It may also be influenced by the stories they have encountered and their own reflection on these. An implication of this is that the study of literature also has a contribution to make to Moral Education.

The contribution that Religious Education can make to the school's programme of sex education needs to be explored in this context, as a specific example of the relationship between Religious and Moral Education. Christianity and the other major world faiths have teachings about the relationship between the sexes, which children will need to be informed about and will need to consider at an appropriate point in their education. Their own experience of life, and their experience of literature and the arts will also provide a basis for reflection and discussion as they grow in understanding. This should not be taken to suggest that all of this will happen in the primary school. Many children will not be ready for such work until they are in secondary school, but there will be some who are already thinking about these things, if only in the context of what they see on television. As a result schools and individual teachers will need to think through their possible responses to children's questions and concerns, and with their governing body formulate school policy and guidelines about this topic. Governors are charged with a legal duty to publish their policy on Sex Education, and teachers should be aware of the nature of such statements in their school.

An opportunity for reflection

> The assembly that morning had been on the creation story in Genesis 1. Over lunch a group of year six boys were sitting with their teacher. One of them opened the conversation with, "You know that story we had in assembly this morning? You don't believe all that rubbish about God making the world in seven days, do you?" "What do you think about it?" was the teacher's reply. This resulted in a lively debate on the subject in which the first boy to speak found that he was forced to reflect, not only on the story itself, but also on his own attitude to it.

Throughout our teaching of Religious Education we must seek to ensure that there is room for our children and young people to reflect on the issues that have been raised, and to explore them in the light of their own experience. For those children who are being brought up in a Christian or other faith by their parents this will have the effect of allowing them to develop and grow in their understanding of that faith. For others it will enable them to explore what it might be like to be a member of a faith community and help them to clarify what they believe. This reflection may happen in the course of classroom activity, or less formally at other times in the school day. It may account for a significant amount of discussion that takes place in the classroom, not directly related to the task in hand. Clearly story can be a strong stimulus to such reflection if the process is not foreclosed by too early an introduction of the "right" answer.

Some types of classroom activity positively encourage reflective discussion. These include group activities such as painting and modelling, drama and certain forms of structured play experiences. Others, particularly those associated with silent activity do not. The atmosphere within the classroom and the school are also important. The school must be a place where children and staff feel safe to be honest about their own thoughts and feelings. This will require that the impact of dominant characters is controlled where this tends to inhibit the contributions of others. Everyone needs to be confident that they will receive the courtesy of attention for their statements of opinion even if these are nonsense, and that if they subsequently change their mind or withdraw their statement this will be respected as part of the process that is essential in coming to an understanding of what others and, perhaps more importantly, what we ourselves think, feel and believe.

While the Religious Education programme provides time for reflection that may enable children to come to understand more fully what they believe, it is not the task of a school in the maintained system of education to seek to bring children to a faith or to nurture them in it. Nor is it the task of a school to undermine a faith in which a child is being nurtured. Religious nurture is the task of the parents and the faith communities. Evangelism is the task of the faith communities. The exception to these general maxims is the Aided school which admits only children from practising Christian homes. These are probably a minority of Church of England Aided schools, but in them some activities identified with Christian nurture may be appropriate.

Religious Education is an exciting and stimulating subject to teach and should be one of the best developed areas in a Church school timetable. This chapter has outlined some aspects of a possible approach to the subject and from this it should be clear that the principal problem is how to fit it all in, and what to leave out. In all this there is little excuse for the repetitious schemes of work that are sometimes a feature of schools that find themselves trapped into following a programme which is tied to the Church's year and other festivals. Repetition is only justified when it is planned to ensure that the children progress in understanding and knowledge as a result of it. Repetition year after year of a festivals approach can create boredom and the impression that religion is all about celebration and nothing else.

Questions for reflection and discussion

1. What are the three most important stories in the Bible for Christians? What place should these have in a Church school's RE programme?
2. How can children be enabled to reflection their experiences of life during the school day?

5

Integration and Balance in the Curriculum

A few years ago while visiting some Church schools I met two boys called Matthew. One was the Matthew mentioned at the beginning of chapter two who was painting a hippopotamus. He was four and a half. The other Matthew was seventeen and a half years old and had just had his first play accepted by the organisers of the Edinburgh Festival Fringe. The difference between these two Matthews is thirteen years, or the school curriculum. The problem for the teacher of the class in which the first Matthew was starting out was to know which one of her charges is the potential playwright.

In the last two chapters some of the specific issues associated with the curriculum in Church schools have been considered. These have presented a partial picture of the curriculum in a Church school, so now a view of the curriculum as a whole must be considered. The introduction of the National Curriculum and other changes introduced in recent years carries with them the danger that schools may lose sight of the overall philosophy underlying their curriculum view under pressure from the need to deal with the myriad detailed documents. In order to restore this balance it is important for schools to take the time to consider possible models for the totality of what children are asked to learn. One model is offered here for consideration and discussion. It is not the only possible one, but it has proved a useful stimulus to discussion on courses and seminars in recent years.

The four strands of the curriculum

There are four distinct threads within the British educational tradition and each needs to be represented within the curriculum of every school. These are

a. *Spiritual*
This is enshrined in the 1988 Education Reform Act, but owes its roots to the history of the Church's involvement in education, beginning with the monasteries. It argues that beyond knowledge there is always something deeper that is unknown, and which can only be perceived through creative reflection on what is known. It speaks to the experience chronicled by David Hay in his paper "The Bearing of Empirical Studies of Religious Experience on Education" and by the project of which he is a member[1]. By allowing that this is an important part of the reality of people's lives it allows for this type of experience to become part of the basis for educational reflection. However it must also relate to the teachings of all the major world faiths, as these are ways in which human beings have responded to their spiritual experience. Christians believe that through Jesus the source and nature of the spiritual was revealed.

b. *Liberal*
This aspect has its roots in the Public and Grammar school traditions, which argue that the educated person is one who has been introduced to and has become familiar with a wide range of human experience, including the humanities and the arts. It is a reminder that education must value the whole person and foster all their talents so that in the end the outcome is a rounded human being.

A combination of these first two threads could be understood to find expression in a phrase from St Paul's letter to the Ephesians (chapter 4, verse 13) "become mature, attaining to the whole measure of the fullness of Christ".

c. *Life Skills*
Essentially practical, this aspect asserts that there are skills which individuals must acquire if they are to be enabled to function within society. University students who are unable to cook themselves a meal are an example of those whose education has omitted this area. For some the acquiring of these skills is so difficult that it becomes the sole object of their education. These skills are not just about survival but include those necessary to make a constructive contribution to a democratic society. Driving a car, filling in forms, budgeting for personal expenditure and sustaining long-term human relationships could all fall within this area and they are neither trivial nor simple skills to acquire.

d. *Technical*
This area has to do with the ability of the young person to earn a living and contribute to the economic development of society. It includes not only a range of skills and a broad area of knowledge but also a set of attitudes that lead the student to regard such activities as important and valuable. It is often argued that the neglect of this area in education has lead to the perceived economic and industrial decline of this country.

Combining these to create the curriculum

It is possible to argue that the parents and wider families of the children in our care should contribute to some of these areas, and some would suggest that this is particulary true of the "Life Skills". Parents will make a significant contribution to their children's education, but this will vary with each home, and so the school must take responsibility for providing a range of educational experiences that cover all four areas. This is not to undervalue the role of parents but to ensure that no assumptions are made that rebound on the child by leaving gaps in their educational experience which could have been filled with more care and planning.

None of these areas is complete and sufficient of itself. The four need to be set in a dynamic tension in order to create a broad and balanced curriculum which meets the needs of the pupils and of society.

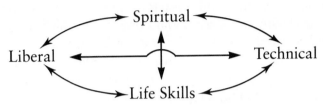

These last two chapters have contained a number of illustrations of the way in which these tensions can be worked through in practice.

> A former colleague, who before entering ordained ministry had been a teacher of music, was having some work done on his retirement home. Visiting it one day he found himself face to face with a former pupil who was the carpenter for the building firm undertaking the work. Recognition was mutual. "I remember you, sir," said the carpenter. "You were the one who taught me to love Sibelius."

How can this be achieved?

If the staff of a school wish to ensure that this model of the curriculum, or another that they have agreed, is carried through into practice, then they will need to give sufficient time to planning and preparation. Accepting the fact that reflection is a key part of the educational experience of the child, we must seek to ensure that as far as possible every part of the school day is used in ways which contribute to the overall aims which have been set. We must make good use of all our resources, human and material, and in particular we must seek to put every part of our school buildings and their grounds to work, even those odd few roses in a bed in the front of the school, which were planted in the days when the sole purpose was to soften the hard lines of the school buildings for neighbours and passers by.

Good planning will lay the framework for achieving more than the attainment targets of the National Curriculum, and will reveal the opportunities that still exist for exploiting the spontaneous within the classroom. When a child brings something in to school on Monday morning to show the other children, and this sparks off a new range of interested enthusiasm, the choice should not be between killing the interest in the service of rigid curriculum planning or abandoning the plan to follow up the interest. Rather the planning should be so thorough that it creates its own flexibility, so that the teacher is enabled to recast the plan to take account of the children's new interest. It will probably require some adjustments to detailed plans and records on Monday evening, but that is part of the professional skill of the teacher.

One of the areas of development that should encourage teachers to retain a broad view of the curriculum is the existence of a national scheme for Records of Achievement. These should contain material which reflects the widest possible range of activity within the curriculum and should include evidence of children's achievements in every area of the school's activity and in the community beyond the school. If they do not, then it will be apparent that the achievements of some children will go unnoted and the school will begin to establish or reinforce the view that only very limited areas of human activity are valuable.

This all sounds very good in theory, but how can it be reflected in practice? Clearly the key is in the planning. By identifying the areas of the Basic Curriculum, that is Religious Education and the National Curriculum, which form the entitlement of every child in a particular group, and then reflecting on these in the light of the broader curriculum principles outlined above or contained in the school's own documentation, it will be possible to identify the ground that should be covered in the period allocated. This can then be broken down into topics, units of work and specific blocks of teaching, ensuring that all the areas to be covered are included and no subject is constantly taught either integrated with something else or in isolation. When these units of teaching have been identified and agreed between staff, then detailed planning can begin. It is at this level that there is a need to retain some flexibility to allow space for the spontaneous. Within this planning there should also be consideration of those children with special educational needs. These may include children whom the teacher knows will find a particular topic or approach difficult or easy, but who otherwise have no generalised special needs.

Questions for discussion or reflection

1. Does the model presented in this chapter provide a helpful basis for discussing balance in the curriculum?
2. Are there other strands in education that should be included in the model?
3. Is there a match between this model and the subjects and cross-curricula themes to be taught in the National Curriculum and Religious Education (the basic curriculum required by the Education Reform Act)?

6

The Hidden Curriculum

School ethos

> The mum was watching her three-year-old playing with the toys that I
> had provided on the floor. She had a baby in a push chair beside her.
> As she had come about arranging for her children to enter the school I
> asked the usual question, "Why do you want your children to come
> to a Church school?" "Well, I - er - well I went to a Church school
> when I was a child and I want that for my children."

Sometimes teachers are as uncertain as this particular mum about
how to explain what makes the difference between a Church
school and others within the maintained sector of the education
system. Sometimes it is described as "being all about sharing and
caring" which can make Church schools sound a bit like a local
supermarket. At other times it has been described as being about
"better discipline" or "teaching them right from wrong". Anyone
who is professionally involved in the work of a Church school
should give some time to reflecting on these issues and so be able to
give a more coherent explanation than these as to what is
distinctive about Church schools in general, and about the one in
which they work in particular. Inevitably such reflection will lead to
a consideration of the ethos of the school and the so- called
"Hidden Curriculum".

The phrase the "hidden curriculum" is used deliberately
although it can be misleading. It is taken to refer to what is learned
by the children as a result of being part of the school community as
opposed to what they learn as a result of the educational

experiences which are being provided in the classroom. This learning should certainly not be "hidden" from the teachers, the governors, or even from the parents. If it is important it should be given careful attention, there should be discussions and documents about it so that everyone knows what is being attempted, how and why.

The ethos of the school is more than just the "hidden curriculum". It is a combination of the worship, the taught curriculum, the extra-curricular activities and the hidden curriculum, which when seen together should combine to become more than the sum of the parts. As there have already been chapters about the curriculum, and there is a chapter later in the book on worship, this chapter will focus on the areas of the school's life which fall outside those two main strands.

The value of the individual

One of the major themes of the gospel is the unique value of individual human beings and their importance in the eyes of God. Within a Church school the basis on which human relationships are built will be this belief. Everyone in the school from the three-year-old just started in the nursery down to the headteacher is a uniquely valuable human being, whom God loves. They are all entitled to the love and respect which that fact demands. Attempting to organise a human institution on that basis can lead to complications.

It is raining at lunchtime, and everyone in the school is in need of more space than is available. Voices are raised in the school hall. You go to investigate the noise and find one of the Dinner Supervisors shouting at a child. There is some food spilt on the floor. The supervisor is claiming that the child threw it there, the child says it was an accident. The supervisor is at screaming point. The child is in tears. A hundred children are looking on. What do you do?

It is much easier to answer the question, if you are not trying to treat each individual as a unique human being loved by God. It takes less time if you do not try to find out why the child and the dinner supervisor had both got into that situation. By giving them time, you may find that you uncover deeper problems than those directly resulting from spilt food, and of course if you uncover problems you will need to take some time over them, even if only to listen.

Naturally there will be occasions when children break rules, are naughty, spiteful or disobedient. In these circumstances the school's approach to discipline will come into play. The principle that seems most appropriate to a Church school is that the children should learn that doing wrong has consequences, which may include punishment, but that following these consequences, there is always forgiveness and reconciliation available. The sin is rejected, but the sinner is not. It is not simply a matter, in every case, of an instant response followed by a cooling off period and then everyone going on as if nothing has happened. This will be appropriate for some of the incidents that happen in the life of the school. At other times there will be more careful consideration and more reflection on the reasons why an offence was committed.

Children need to be provided with a secure framework of expected behaviour, within which they can operate, and against which they can sometimes press. Therefore there will need to be some rules and these will need to be explicit to all in the school and as far as is possible consistently applied. At some time all children will break these rules, either through inattention, bravado or a deliberate attempt to establish whether the rules are still being upheld. This is normal behaviour, and is usually easily dealt with. However there are two groups of children about whom teachers should be concerned. These are:

a. those children who never break the rules;

b. those children who break them so often that it seems to be a habit that the ordinary school sanctions cannot alter.

Rule keeping and rule breaking

If there are children who never seem to be in trouble, who never break a rule, it should cause teachers to reflect on those children's attitudes to school, and to the world. It may be that they are so frightened and inhibited that they do not dare to let themselves become involved in anything that might lead them to stray even close to the theoretical line between acceptable and unacceptable behaviour. If that is true then perhaps teachers should be exploring ways in which these children can be encouraged to be bolder. Teachers might even be led to rejoice if they find that they are punishing one of these children, as this could be a sign of progress. It may be that their homes are so strict or inhibited that they dare not do anything not directly sanctioned by an adult. At least teachers should know if this is part of some children's backgrounds. It may be of course that there exists one class in the country that contains angels, whose nature is to be perfect in all things but extensive school visiting has failed to identify such paragons.

It is more likely that any class contains some of the other group, whose natural position on the continuum from acceptable to unacceptable behaviour seems to be considerably beyond the unacceptable end. For such children it will be important that teachers have an understanding of what causes them to behave as they do, if only so that there can be developed a response to the children's behaviour that is consistent and that carries with it some potential for improvement. Perhaps their experience of life outside school has been or still is so bad that they are unable to control their response to it in school. For these children perhaps the greatest good that teachers can do is to provide them with a consistent, loving framework inside school, which by the security that it offers gives them a break from the pressures of the world outside. For the child who knows that its mother is dying, a school cannot provide a cure for the hurt, but it can provide a secure place to which the hurt can be brought, and which is prepared to listen to the pain.

Other children may break the rules as a way of seeking attention. The logic of the behaviour of these children is that they need to be given attention in ways that do not reinforce the bad behaviour. Therefore it will be important to ensure that when they behave in ways which are acceptable, or when they complete tasks at a good standard for them they should be praised for that. You do not prevent attention-seeking behaviour by denying a person attention. Yet other children may have learned antisocial patterns of behaviour in the world outside school; they will need help, support and encouragement if they are to learn to live within alternative standards to those to which they have already become accustomed.

All of this may sound to some as if bad behaviour is being explained and therefore excused. This is not the case. Bad behaviour is always to be rejected, but in rejecting it we do not reject the child who has perpetrated it, rather we attempt to help them to come to accept that there are better ways to behave.

A school discipline policy should always be designed to provide a basis of self-discipline. If it becomes too dependent on the staff enforcing the acceptable standards, then it does not carry the seeds of further growth to maturity. It only has within it the seeds of increased dependency. This implies that there must always be trust. It is only by being trusted that we learn to be trusted. Within a school where every human being is accorded that respect shown to unique human beings loved by God, this should come naturally, and where there are failures, as there will be, these can be dealt with not as disasters but as experience from which learning can grow.

Things of value

Chris was not very good at writing any type of consecutive English, so when he came up with a story that was quite interesting and well written, and was the best piece of work that he had done all year, it was natural that he should be asked to read it in assembly. Knowing that he was not a fluent reader, he was offered the option of having someone else read his story, but he insisted on doing it himself. He read it very badly, and there was some embarrassed shuffling amongst the older children. At the end of the assembly he approached the headteacher.

"That wasn't very good, was it," he said. "No, I'm afraid it wasn't, Chris." "I'll do it much better next time," he said, and walked off reasonably content.

The "hidden curriculum" is not just about discipline and relationships, it is also about the things that the school values, and how these things are valued. If you examine the displays at your school, and listen to what is mentioned in assembly, and what is omitted, you will quickly form an impression of what seems to be important to the school.

Sometimes an aspect of school life, very good in itself, may be in conflict with the values of the school as a whole.

Some years ago while working as part of a diocesan education team I wrote a short leaflet about Halloween in which I argued, I thought clearly and convincingly, that Church schools should think very carefully before including this topic in their curriculum for the autumn term. It was published in early September by the diocese in which I was working. Shortly before half-term I was visiting a Church primary school in the diocese. I walked into one classroom which was covered in witches, pumpkins, broomsticks and magic spells. Somewhat hesitantly I asked the teacher why she had chosen this topic. "Oh," she said, "we had this interesting booklet from the diocese about it."

Some schools seem to value success in absolute terms, but give little attention to doing the best that we can. Some schools value beauty highly, but never seem to acknowledge that the imperfect may still be of value. Some schools value order and tidiness, others a working environment in which an element of clutter enables a stream of production. High achievement may be praised in music, sport or art but is it ever mentioned in connection with mathematics or science?

> At the end of assembly in the village school the headteacher gave an account of the participation of the school gymnastics team in an inter-school competition on the previous evening. Particular praise was given to a child who had volunteered to take part at the last minute to "make up the numbers" thus enabling the team to enter at all, despite the fact that everyone in the school knew that the child had the greatest difficulty in completing a forward roll. As the report continued everyone became proud of what the school had done at the competition in which they had been by far the smallest school represented. In this context it hardly seemed to matter that the team had come last in the competition.

A further explicit part of the life of the school that reveals its values is the way in which it approaches those children who have special educational needs. Some schools still seem to see these as a discrete group who find learning generally difficult or who have an obvious identifiable handicap, and therefore are in constant need of extra help. If this is the only possible approach in their circumstances then such schools will need to be very careful about how these children are helped to develop their own sense of worth within the community, which is part of the process of coming to know that you are valued by it. However other schools remain closer to the understanding of Special Education Needs that underpinned the 1981 Education Act. These schools will see many children as having special educational needs at some point in their school career, perhaps in only one quite specific area of learning. Such an approach, being more inclusive, is easy to incorporate into the ethos of a Church school. A third group of schools, will see the needs wider still, and will argue that everyone, being unique, will have special needs that the school must attempt to meet, even if these are only needing to learn how to succeed, or how to fail without doing so much of the latter that the experience becomes destructive. In such schools the real progress of every child will be monitored and guided on a personal basis. At its best the National Curriculum framework can provide a valuable tool for this.

Logically following from this is the way that the school responds to the needs of those outside its own community. What policies are there within a school towards the involvement of children in charitable activity? Are these consistent with the educational and philosophical priorities that the school expresses within its own community? How do children learn to give expression to the compassion that they feel for those less fortunate than themselves in ways that develop the response into adult maturity?

If the children are to learn that they are all valued and loved for who they are, then they need to become confident that their achievements and their contribution to the life of the school will be noted, respected and given worth by the attention paid to them. This is one of the reasons why the principles that lie behind the development of the Records of Achievement Schemes are so much to be welcomed.

A therapeutic community

As schools develop towards a community based on the gospel there will be times when under the pressure of the complexity of the task some limits are sought. Of course the school must be an educational community, but must it also seek to be a therapeutic community? The answer to this must inevitably be yes, if a therapeutic community is one which cares for more of the individual than the inculcation of knowledge into the mind. If it is to be a therapeutic community, are there limits to this? Must it extend to parents and staff as well as children? Every headteacher will know that one of the greatest demands on their time and energy is the work that they do with parents. They also know that much of this is vital to the well-being of the children, and therefore to their education. If there have to be limits perhaps it is that the school must be a therapeutic community for the child, and for the parent where this does not prevent it working for the child, and for the staff where this does not prevent it working for the child and the parent.

The whole of this chapter has taken as its framework the gospel teaching about the relationships appropriate between human beings in a Christian community. This example of the Christian life in action should become explicit to the parents, and perhaps also to some at least of the children. It may be that this happens most naturally in the context of worship, but it may also emerge when the school has to explain the stands that it takes on some issues.

> I was recently visiting a school which served a deprived housing estate. The headteacher told me that it was the normal behaviour in the area for children to take their weapons to school with them. The first task of the school was to ensure that such weapons did not come onto school premises, and then to ensure that within those premises the relationships were conducted on a basis other than "get your blow in first". This needed explanation to the parents, and this provided the opportunity to ensure that the parents understood the gospel basis on which the school was organised.

Attempting to develop the life of the school as a community in the light of the gospel is no soft option. It takes time, energy, commitment and determination. It may not lead to the school taking action that is different from that taken by the county school down the road, but the basis for that action is the theological undergirding that the gospel provides.

Questions for reflection and discussion

1. Which children's behaviour gives you most cause for concern? How can you plan a policy to help such children?
2. On what things should a Church school community place the highest value?

7

Worship and Assembly

The legal position

The 1988 Education Reform Act requires that every child must be involved in an act of worship on each school day. Within Church schools this must be conducted in accordance with the Trust Deed, which will almost certainly refer to the practice and traditions of the Church of England. The challenge to Church primary schools is to ensure that these legal requirements are met in ways which also reflect the needs of the child and the ethos of the school. This is no easy task. Few priests have to prepare at least five acts of worship every week without the support of a liturgical framework. It is made more complicated by the limited amount of time that schools seem to be able to commit to the preparation and planning of worship. Too often it is left to the headteacher to do on her own, while the rest of the staff complain that the results are boring. The preparation of a lively, interesting contemplative, prayerful programme of worship for the children is a task on which all teachers and governors need to engage together.

Understanding worship?

A further complication is the demand made by some educationalists that the children must understand what they are doing if they are going to be asked to do it. This demand sits uncomfortably within a faith which has at its heart the mystery of the Eucharist. Few adult Christians would claim to understand this, but it does not prevent them from joining in the celebration of the mystery on a regular basis. Nor can we accept the argument that says that because not all children may be worshipping when they attend worship in school we should not offer them the opportunity to do so. Not all adult worshippers are worshipping during the whole of the service that they attend on Sunday. It does not prevent them from coming, nor the minister from offering them the opportunity to worship when they are there. The basis of school worship is that during an individual act of worship some of those present will be worshipping, some will be experiencing something approaching worship, others will be finding out what it might be like to worship, and there are no enquiries made about who was doing what. In the course of this, as a result of the varied pattern of worship offered by the school, those who are worshipping will have their experience of worship broadened, and those who are not worshipping will be finding out what it is like to worship by being with those who are. Both of these results are educational in a broad sense, and therefore a valid objective for a school.

There will come a time in the development of all children when they will wish to discuss whether they believe in what they are being asked to do. When that time comes it should be clear that if they do not feel that they can honestly participate at the moment, they have the option of not participating, provided that they do not disrupt those who are. This is not and must not be made into a once and for all decision. It can only be conditional and subject to review and change by the child.

Planning worship

There are a number of stages to this task and if one or more are omitted then it is likely that the resultant programme will fail to meet the expectations that are held for it.

Initially it will be necessary to ensure that everyone involved has some shared understanding of the variety of views of worship and what it might contain that are held within the school. If you gather a group of adults together and ask them to talk about their experience of worship and which aspects they find most or least helpful, you will almost certainly find that they first attended church with a member of their family, that they most clearly remember those acts of worship in which they were directly involved, usually the ones associated with rites of passage and that if they go to church as adults it is with their partner, their children or on their own. After that agreement ceases. Some like the old hymns, some like modern music, and for some music prevents worship. Some can only worship in a church building, while others prefer to worship almost anywhere else. Some find sermons helpful, while many find them boring. Some value the Book of Common Prayer, while others prefer the Alternative Service Book or improvised worship. Some have no contact with worship at all outside school. There is likely to be no consensus which would enable someone to design an act of worship which would be entirely satisfactory for all present. Public worship inevitably carries with it an element of compromise. Perhaps one of the reasons that we find coming together within the Churches so difficult and frustrating is that we do not admit either the extent to which we already compromise our preferences in worship, or the limits that we are prepared to set to further compromise.

If organising an act of worship for a dozen adults will involve them all in some give and take, and acceptance of activity which they do not find helpful, how much more difficult it is to organise an act of worship for perhaps a hundred children so that they are not only helped to worship, or to approach worship now, but also helped to grow in their understanding of what worship is and what it may include.

Having accepted that we are dealing with a complex task, it is now appropriate to attempt some simplification in order to establish basic principles and also to distinguish between worship and assembly.

Worship involves many things including coming together to praise God, to pray to him and to hear his word and then to depart. It could be represented in a diagram like this.

Assembly involves coming together, activity which focuses on the life and values of the community, and then departing. It could be represented in a diagram like this.

Naturally this is grossly over-simplified and the theologians and liturgists will be deeply offended by it, but I hope that it makes a significant point about the difference between worship and assembly. Assembly is a valid and often important activity in schools, as it is a major opportunity to make explicit, assert or celebrate the values of the school. However to do that without the focus on God, and without the opportunity for him to speak is to do something which is not worship.

> "Thank you, class five, for telling us all about your topic on light. We all really enjoyed it. Shall we give them a clap. Now I'm afraid that we don't have time for a hymn this morning, but perhaps class five could sing their song about a lamplighter again, while we all go back to our classes."

While the diagrams shown here are clearly limited it is probably helpful to press them just a little further in order to reflect on the activities that could be included in each section of an act of worship.

Coming together

> It was during the Easter season, that is the period between the festival of Easter and Ascension Day that I visited the school to join them for their worship. As the children entered the hall the headteacher played a piece of recorded music. He chose for that day an excerpt from Carmina Burana by Carl Orff. It was particularly familiar to me as the choral society to which I belong had it in rehearsal at the time, so although it was being sung in old German I knew the subject of the section that was being played. Fortunately it was not one of the sections on the joys of sexual love, but it was about the joys of gambling. The music is good. It is exciting and direct in its appeal. Did it matter that it was on a profane subject?

As the children come into the area that is to be used for worship there needs to be something about that area that signals that it is now being used for worship, and not for Physical Education or eating lunch. This may be done by having a small table or candles or a cross which is placed as a focal point in the room or hall only when worship is to take place. It may be done by having some of the furniture placed in a way that is only used for worship. Suitable music may be played to encourage the children to enter quietly, and to aid their concentration on the activity to come. The children should know where they are expected to be in the room and whether they should sit or stand. When everyone is gathered the person who is going to lead the worship should greet the children. Most commonly this seems to be by saying "Good morning" or "Good afternoon". It may well be that this is a point where the use of appropriately chosen versicles and responses can have the merit of introducing not only greater variety into the worship but also some elements of the Anglican liturgical tradition. These could be taken from either the Book of Common Prayer or the Alternative Service Book, both of which should be available in every Church of England school as part of the resources for worship.

Being a community

"I'd like some volunteers to help me with assembly next week," said the vicar..

Several hands shot up. When I overheard the word "pets" in the quiet discussion between the volunteers and the vicar after assembly I should have known. Next week a dog, a cat, a large rabbit, two gerbils, a guinea pig, a hamster and three goldfish were brought into the hall. It was an exciting time. The dog was interested in everything that moved, especially the cat, the rabbit and the five-year-olds in the front row.

"Sorry about that," said the vicar to the caretaker afterwards, as a calling card was removed from the hall floor. What could anyone say? Who, but the caretaker could complain? The school took until break time to settle down again, but as a community we had shared our concern and care for our pets and everyone had enjoyed it so much.

As the school, or a large part of it, meets together it is natural that there are things that children and teachers will want to share. This aspect of worship is where the hidden curriculum is given tangible expression. It has its parallels in the peace, the offertory and the notices in church worship. It can be a time when, as a group, we rejoice in the things that are good, and sometimes also give expression to our sorrows. It will be this aspect of the worship or assembly that ensures that it is always relevant to the experience of the child.

Praising and praying

In the school where I was a headteacher there was a tradition of a Friday afternoon assembly to which children could bring any good work, news, reports of activities or requests for support which they wished to communicate to the school as a whole. To close this assembly I would then attempt to link the various themes together by focusing them in prayer. After some years of doing this my deputy approached me one day and said, "Don't you think that it would be a good idea if the children wrote the prayers for Friday afternoons?" Ever willing to delegate tasks I agreed, and the quality instantly improved. This was achieved, because the children did not attempt to reflect the activities that were being reported, but rather prayed about the week that had just passed in school, thus creating a much broader and more appropriate context.

Within this area of activity will be included singing, including hymns from all generations of church worship, as well as those that are particulary written to enable children to worship, dance, and prayers of adoration, thanksgiving, confession, penitence and petition for others and for ourselves. It is important that over a number of acts of worship this range and balance is maintained, and no apology is made for listing the different types of prayer. Most schools encourage children to write their own prayers and this is important, but it does not help them to learn to do this well if they do not become familiar not only with prayers of petition, that is prayers that ask God for something, but also prayers of adoration (praise), thanksgiving, confession and penitence. The use of the liturgical material from the two prayer books and the great prayers from every generation will not only help the children to become familiar with these different types of prayer, but will also develop points of contact for them with the worship used in churches. This is part of the educational task of school worship in that it gives the children an experience of what worship is like, and also retains the possibility that they may become worshipping adults.

Listening to God

This should be more than just listening to a story or a reading. It may include drama, presentations on slide, videotape or overhead projectors, and visiting speakers, and must from time to time include silence, either in the form of silent prayer or quiet moments of reflection. If we do not stop talking, how can we expect God to get a word into the conversation?

> The best assembly that I ever saw was one which focused on silent prayer. It had been carefully prepared and a worshipful atmosphere had been created. The teacher, not a headteacher, who led the worship then carefully explained that silent prayer was about listening carefully as well as thinking about those things that you wanted God to know. As the silence that she had introduced continued it became more and more profound. No-one could bring themselves to break into it. At last after some minutes, the noise of the school cook dropping something in the kitchen broke in, and with great reluctance we all came back to the ordinary world of school. It was one of those occasions when the adults in the room were really worshipping with the children, not just leading them in worship. I should make the point that this act of worship took place in a medium sized primary school with all age groups present.

Going out

If a worshipping atmosphere has been created, as it was in the example on silent prayer, then the way in which the children leave the room becomes important. There should be a clear ending to the worship, perhaps using one of a number of well known short prayers or words of dismissal. Then after a moment or two of quiet the children should begin to leave the room. They should know how they are expected to leave, so that it can be achieved without the need to give too many instructions. It should be done in an orderly way, and possibly accompanied by well chosen music. Unless it is absolutely unavoidable all children should leave the room, even if one of the classes is to use the room for their next lesson, so that there is a clear signal that the formal act of worship is over.

The content of worship

All that has been covered so far in this chapter has looked at the mechanics of worship and its planning. It has not yet addressed the content of the worship.

There are many schools which use either published assembly books or the Church's year to provide a framework within which to identify the content of worship. The problem that both of these approaches leave unaddressed is the relevance that the worship has to the rest of the life of the school and of the children and staff within it. If worship is to be interesting and varied and if it is to retain the children's attention then it must be well integrated into the life of the school. This can be achieved by seeking to relate the content of the worship to the themes and topics that are the focus of work in the classroom. Thus as the staff meet together to plan their work for the coming term or year they should also be planning their worship themes to relate to this. Sometimes the worship may be used as the starting point for a topic or theme, at other times it may be used to give the work going on in several classes a particular focus. Alongside this curriculum led approach will be the major festivals in the Church's year, and possibly some from other faiths represented in the school. This can be used to develop a programme of worship for the term or year. Some schools even plan their worship in outline for longer periods than this. Once the plan has been developed in outline the detail can be filled in.

At a staff meeting the topic of worship in the school was raised. Several members of staff admitted that they found leading worship very difficult, but were unable to identify why this should be as they were quite confident in their approach to their own class, or to larger groups in the school. At last the truth began to dawn. The problem that they were experiencing was not associated with the numbers of children present, or the nature of worship. It had to do with the other members of staff. "It would be all right if the staff weren't there," said one teacher summing up the feelings of many. It was agreed that it would not be right for the staff to withdraw, as their presence was important for the children and for themselves. However it was agreed that everyone would attempt to be much more supportive of the leaders of worship, by ensuring that they set an example of careful attention to the worship, that their body language was supportive and encouraging, not critical, and that comments after worship were kept constructive. They also agreed that they would assist in the leadership more in order to move away from the idea that only one teacher at a time was involved in the leadership of worship.

This did not instantly solve the problem, but over time all the teachers found it becoming easier to lead worship, and so confidence grew.

Some acts of worship will become the responsibility of a class or group of children, helped by their teacher, some will be led by the teachers on their own or in groups, some will be led by the headteacher and some by the parish clergy. Others may also be involved in leadership or planning. All should know how the act of worship that they are to lead will fit into the overall plan, and should be familiar with the prayers and songs which are known to the children, or which are going to be introduced to them in the near future. It is important that this basic repertoire of worship material is well known to all the leaders, is kept under review and is constantly renewed. It is very helpful to both the children and the overall work of the parish in which the school is based or which it serves if this repertoire has some areas of overlap with that used in the worship of the parish.

Within this overall plan the school may also wish to organise some celebrations of the Eucharist. When this is done and how regularly will depend in part on the traditions within the parish in which the school works, but the same general principles will apply to planning a school Eucharist as the other acts of worship that have been the focus here.

None of this planning and organisation will guarantee uniformly superb acts of worship for every child every day, but it should ensure that their experience of worship in school is not just the minimum sufficient to immunise them against the real thing for life.

Questions for reflection and discussion

1.How can you establish the extent of the experience of worship which the children bring with them to school?

2.How can you ensure that the programme of worship in a school is well planned and resourced?

3. How can you ensure that everyone in a school is involved in the leadership of worship? Would it be appropriate if they were?

8

Involving the Parish

Visiting the local church

"I have just phoned the vicar of St Adam's," said my deputy. "I wanted to arrange for my class to go to visit his church, next month. I am absolutely furious."

"Why, wouldn't he let you come?"

"No, he said we could come any time on the Tuesday. He would leave the church key under a flower pot by the porch, and would we be sure to put it back after we had locked up. You would have thought that he might at least have offered to meet us there."

Fortunately teachers and their classes receive a warmer welcome than that from most of the churches that they wish to visit. A Church school, of course has an advantage in that its close contacts with the parish enable it to make the fullest possible use of the church buildings to benefit the children's education, always assuming that the church is close by and that it is not in use for other purposes. This does mean that visits by classes to the church can be carefully prepared and do not have to attempt to do everything at once. One visit could be organised in connection with a history topic, to use the building for its historical links. Another might be in connection with art, to look at the stained glass, or the carvings, and inevitably there will be many visits in connection with themes from Religious Education. In the course of these visits the children should begin to establish not only a familiarity with the building but also some understanding of what it is used for and how it is used. Indeed many Church schools will use the church for acts of worship themselves, and may join the congregation there for special occasions. Assuming there is space it is always good to invite members of the congregation to join the school at worship when it is using the church for a mid-week service.

However the local church is not just the building, it is also the community who use it and who care for it. Naturally the children are most likely to meet the vicar or rector and the other parish clergy if there are any. They are likely to be frequent visitors to school, and hopefully will soon become recognised by the children away from the school setting.

The parish clergy

The headteacher and the parish priest were sitting in the head's study having a cup of coffee and talking to me about their working relationship. The headteacher was also the parish organist.

"It's quite simple," said the head, "When I am in the church playing the organ, I am working for him." "And," said the vicar, "when I am in school taking assembly, or teaching year six, I am working for her."

The parish clergy are an important personal resource to the school. They may be used to lead worship, to teach religious education, to help in planning both these areas of work or even to assist in other curriculum areas. Not every priest will be good at or feel comfortable doing all of these and it is a wise school that makes sure that they have discussed with each member of the clergy what he or she feels they are able to do best and are most comfortable with, and so make best use of the time that they can give. There are some who make their most important contribution by taking the children for football or leading a computer club. Others may be most appreciated for the way in which they ensure that they are available to the staff and support them. Sometimes they can be persuaded to join school trips and visits as a helper. However it is most common to find them making their contribution to the worship and Religious Education.

Support for RE and worship

I was leading a staff discussion on Religious Education. The Rector of the parish, then in his seventies, was present. We had got on to the topic of progression in Religious Education, and I was talking about the problem of ensuring that there was deepening of the children's understanding year by year when the major festivals were the focus of the work.

"How can you make sure that your children will learn something new about Christmas this year?" I asked.

"Well," said the Rector, "I understand the point that you are making, but for me it is very simple. You see I learn something new about the festival every year, and I try to share that with those who I am teaching."

Not all clergy are comfortable teaching young children. No-one should feel that they are forced to take on tasks in which they are certain that they will fail. However they do have particular insights to contribute to the planning and delivery of the Religious Education programme, and it may be that their most helpful work will be done by joining the staff for their discussions about this area of the curriculum. By the same token their understanding and knowledge of worship is also an important resource. They will normally be involved in the planning of worship and may undertake a regular leadership role. However it should not be assumed that they will only attend school worship when they are going to lead it. Sometimes they may wish to sit with the staff and the children and enjoy being a participant. The occasion at which they must be present as leader will be when the school holds a Eucharist, if this is part of the school's pattern of worship.

Other roles for the parish clergy

There are so many things that a parish priest may do in a Church school, quite apart from their role on the governing body, that schools must beware of creating too many demands. There must be a clear understanding of what is to be attempted. Perhaps one of the most important objectives is to ensure that there is time for the clergy to join the staff for coffee in the staff room sufficiently regularly for them to be known as human beings and colleagues. The test here is does the person making the coffee have to ask "How do you take your coffee, vicar?" If that question has to be asked, or if there is a feeling that we have to find the vicar the best mug, then he has not yet become a sufficiently regular visitor to have become a colleague and friend. When this stage has been achieved then he is probably also in a position to fulfil the other aspect of his role in the school, that of pastor and chaplain to the staff. Such a role includes befriending all the staff, not just the teachers, and the children of the school, perhaps following models drawn from industrial chaplaincy. Teaching or working with children can be such a demanding activity that someone who both knows the school and is well known within it can provide a most valuable support when things are difficult, tiring or apparently unsuccessful. Equally a person who can share the joys of the work and ensure that those who have contributed to moments of individual or group success are thanked by someone other than the headteacher is an important member of the community.

The parish community

However the church is not just the buildings and the clergy. It is also the worshipping community. The parish needs to know about its school, and needs to feel involved in it. Therefore the school will need to ensure that communication with the parish is always under consideration. Sometimes the links are given formal expression, by the headteacher being automatically a member of the Parochial Church Council, or the school making regular contributions to the parish magazine, perhaps of children's work. Although this needs careful co-ordination the school should attempt to ensure that it makes its appropriate contribution to the celebration of the festivals in church, and possibly to the fund raising activities and socials. Perhaps the school's country dance group will do a display at the fete, or the choir sing some carols at one of the Christmas services. A special focus may be made of Education Sunday, which comes each year shortly before the start of Lent, with the school contributing to the service, and perhaps a visiting preacher, who will speak on a subject related to the Church's role in education.

There will be some people in the parish who will ask questions about what the church gets out of having a Church school. These may be people who see the church contributing money to the governors' funds and who want to know what "value" they are getting for it. Fortunately there is now research evidence available which demonstrates the benefits to the parish of having a Church school. This has been reported in publications from the National Society and those schools who are members of the Society will have the relevant publications available. There may also be people who still think that the parish's responsibility to assist the parents in nurturing their children in the Christian faith is fulfilled by the school. For such people there needs to be a continuing dialogue to help them to understand the difference between nurture and education, and to see that the experience that children receive as a result of being members of a Sunday school or Church choir is complementary to that which they receive by attending a Church school.

Confirmation classes?

A particular issue which will arise in some parishes is the relationship between the Church school and the confirmation class. Confirmation is an important milestone in the process of Christian nurture. Every parish will have its own view of the appropriate age for confirmation. This will reflect among other things the worshipping tradition in the parish. In those parishes where the Eucharist (or Communion) is the main service each week, it is probable that children will be confirmed at a younger age than they will in a parish which uses Morning and Evening Prayer as their principal service. In eucharistically based parishes there is a greater likelihood that there will be school celebrations of the Eucharist. In such parishes some may suggest that confirmation preparation should be offered in or based at the school. While there are arguments on both sides, it is likely that this will only be seen as appropriate in school where it is possible to assume that all the parents are involved in the church community. Care will need to be taken in these cases to ensure that everyone is convinced that holding a school based confirmation class will not give the children the impression that the responsibilities of full membership of the Church are left behind when school is left. A further argument against school based confirmations is that it is difficult to see how the necessary follow up to early confirmation can be sustained, if it has been primary school based. For the vast majority of Church schools therefore confirmation will be parish based, although the school may well wish to join with the celebration when children who attend the school are confirmed.

The relationships between the Church school and its parish provide many opportunities for the school to receive important support. They also provide the parish with many opportunities to make contact with parents and children. These are mutually beneficial and while the relationship will always need work the results are usually rewarding and strengthening.

Questions for reflection and discussion

1. What roles could the parish clergy play in the life of the Church school that you know best?
2. What support would they need in order to be able to fulfil these roles?

9

Involving Parents

The welcoming school

I walked into the school. There was an attractive display in a corner of the entrance. The whole area looked clean and tidy, and I could just hear from along the corridor the gentle noises of a school at work. On my left, clearly signed was the secretary's office. There was a door marked "Do not enter" and a sliding glass panel. The panel was in the closed position. Beside the panel was a bell push. Hoping that it was not the fire alarm I pushed it. I could make out a figure on the other side of the frosted glass. After what seemed a long time the figure came over to the panel and opened it.

"Yes?" said the lady.

"I have an appointment to see the headteacher," I said, and gave my name.

"Wait there, I will see if she has time to see you." The panel closed.

For some time the figure moved about on the other side of the panel, and then left the room presumably through a door that connected with the headteacher's office. A moment later the headteacher emerged.

"Hello, David. How nice to see you. Would you like a coffee."

I rarely refuse free coffee.

"Could we have two coffees, please, Mrs Smith?" said the head.

The lady who had first addressed me through the glass panel, now identified as Mrs Smith, smiled broadly and asked me if I would like milk and sugar in my coffee.

The first thing that a parent sees of the inside of a school is the entrance hall, the secretary's room and the headteacher's room. The first people that they meet are usually the secretary, the headteacher and sometimes the caretaker. These encounters are the start of a relationship which must be expected to last seven years or even longer if there is more than one child in the family. From the first the experience should be one that reflects the gospel. The way in which the entrance area is organised and material displayed in it should speak of the school's values. These opening meetings in the future relationship should reflect the way in which the school understands the need to regard everyone as being made in the image of God. Therefore it is worth taking a little time and trouble to ensure that the right basis for the relationship is created and that things get off to a good start.

Information about the school

Of course the parents will already have some impressions of the school formed from the comments of other parents, the behaviour of the children from the school when they are in the street and possibly from contacts through the Church. They may also have obtained a copy of the school's Information for Parents brochure. The school is required by the 1980 Education Act to publish this each year and some of its contents are determined by law. However despite its legalistic origins it can be a useful means of presenting the school and the values for which it stands. Every teacher should read their school's brochure from time to time. It can make revealing reading. For instance, is what it says about Sex Education something that matches with the school policy documents and what happens in the classroom? Apart from comments on Sex Education the brochure must contain the school's admissions policy, and many details about the organisation of the school and of the curriculum.

The key relationship – the early years

All of these aspects of the initial contact with parents contribute to the first impression. However, in the long term, perhaps the key relationships are those created between the parents and the teachers of the first two or three classes that the children attend. If these are good then a sound basis has been created for the long term. If these are poor then it becomes almost impossible for the school to recover the lost ground. Once parents begin to learn that they are not welcome, or that the teachers have no time for them, then the principal means by which parents learn about the school and its values has become the gossip at the school gate. Good relationships in these early years depend on a close and open relationship between the parents and the teachers.

> As the parents came into the room they were asked if they would like tea or coffee. There were toys for the children to play with. The headteacher and the reception class teacher were both there looking relaxed, and chatting to the newcomers. When all had arrived the head welcomed everyone, and said a few words about how the children would be admitted to the school.
> "Oh, by the way," she said, "do give a thought to what you are going to do on the first day. Of course, you can stay in the classroom as long as you like, but you may find that your child walks straight into the room with hardly a pause to say, "'Bye mum", leaving you standing there feeling like a spare part. Particularly if this is your last child to come in you may find that when you get back to your home it feels very quiet and empty. You may be looking forward to the peace and quiet, but it might be a good idea if you know a friend with whom you can go and have a coffee if it feels too lonely."

Building confidence

One of the ways in which the communications between the school and the parents can be undermined is if the impression is created that the teachers are not confident in what they are doing. This is where all the hours of staff discussion and all the time spent on courses can have an important benefit. If as a result of a continuing commitment to further study and close work with colleagues, teachers are able to speak well and clearly about the work that they are doing with the children in ways that the parents can understand then it is likely that the parents will support them. This of course implies that the teachers are able to explain the theoretical basis of their work to the parent who puts the petrol in their cars at the local garage and the parent who designed the car in the first place. It is not sufficient for the headteacher alone to be able to talk like this with parents, for it is not the headteacher who will be teaching their children for the majority of their time in school, unless the school is very small.

Parents' evenings are one of the key forums for these discussions, whether they are of the "Come and discuss your child's progress" or the "Come and discuss how we teach Maths" type of evening. In terms of passing on detailed information about how Johnny is doing with his spelling they have their limitations, and such discussions probably need to happen at other times, but their greater value is in conveying the basic message that the staff are competent both in practice and in their understanding of the theory that lies behind it.

Written communication is also important. The tone of letters written to parents needs to be carefully monitored so that it also reflects the messages that the school wishes to convey. There also need to be some checks that such letters are getting through.

"We have agreed that in future all letters sent out to parents of every child in the school will be numbered, so that if you receive number five and the previous one that you had was number two you will know that some have gone missing. If we work together I am sure that we can make sure that most of the letters that we send out to you via your child reach you, but can I suggest that you take the basic precaution of checking the contents of your children's trouser pockets before you put them into the washing machine. I know that we have found several important letters from our own children's school in this way, and it's better to find them then rather than after they have been through the machine."

As well as letters home there must now be an annual report. This is a further opportunity to provide good quality communication if the attempt is made to write something that reflects the child, and does not get trapped into trite phrases. If a teacher cannot think of anything more than "Could do better", has this teacher really been treating the child as a unique human being made in the image of God for a whole year?

Caring for parents

"Can I have a word with you?"

"Of course," said the headteacher.

"I am very worried about Jane. Ever since her husband has left home she has been looking very thin and drawn. There never seems to be any food in the house. I think that there may be money problems. I wonder if she is getting the benefits that she should."

"I agree but what do you want me to do about it?"

"Do you think that you could have a word with her? She wouldn't take it from me."

As was mentioned in a previous chapter the school has a role in the support of the parents. This may be expressed by giving parents time to listen to their concerns about their children, or it may be more general. When parents begin to have confidence in the school in this area, then conversations such as the one recorded above may take place. It is probable that the class teacher would be unaware of this conversation or the action that the headteacher took in response to the request, but in a school where there is mutual trust between parents and teachers and the teachers are known to be concerned about the welfare of the children and families with whom they are in contact, it should be assumed that such incidents occur.

Many schools will have some agreed action in order to ensure that when a member of staff becomes committed to dealing with a particular problem the normal working of the school is not disrupted. This will probably start from the assumption that the parent has the right to choose to whom they wish to speak. This may not always be the headteacher. As far as possible when Mrs Smith comes to the school in tears to say to the member of staff she trusts most, that her life is falling apart, that member of staff should be freed to listen and to offer what immediate help she can. Perhaps she has come to the school secretary, who has taken her into the headteacher's room where they can speak in confidence. If this means that the headteacher makes them both a cup of tea and then gets on with the dinner numbers, then that should be as normal as it would be if it was the headteacher who was speaking to Mrs Smith and the secretary providing the tea. Equally, if it is a class teacher who is selected, then that teacher's class should be covered. This also implies that members of staff support each other in coping with the stress that can be created by being the person to whom those in trouble turn.

Parental help in school

Most relationships with parents do not involve providing a listening ear in times of crisis. For much of the time the school will look to the benefits to the children's education that can be derived from good relations with the parents. This may be direct and take the form of parents helping in the classroom, with escorting children on trips out, and in organising or making resources for the school. Where parents help in these ways, particularly if they are working with the children, it will be important that they understand and share something of the school's approach to the care of children, and the type of relationships between children that the school is attempting to foster. The benefit may be more indirect as the school benefits from the skills of the parents as they raise funds for the school or help within the governing body with the school's management.

In accepting these forms of help the school is not only benefiting directly, but it may also be benefiting for the growth in personal development of individual parents that arises from their being given the opportunities to exercise their talents in new ways. There will be many schools which experience mixed emotions on finding that their most regular parent volunteers are suddenly announcing that they will no longer be able to help at the school as they have now obtained paid employment. This may have a significant affect on the finances of the family; the school, far from being upset, should perhaps feel satisfied that it has helped in the process of generating the confidence necessary to enable the parent to return to work.

Appointments with the headteacher

"Of course we welcome parents into the school. My door is always open. Parents can come and see me whenever they like."

Many schools have a policy like this in relation to their parents. The interesting test to apply to it is "How many parents have come through the open door?" Not all parents are sufficiently confident to walk into their child's school and ask to see the headteacher immediately. Indeed sometimes the "open door" policy is in reality very heavily qualified. "Parents can come and see me whenever they like provided that I am in school, am not teaching, and am not tied up with someone else" is probably how it works out in practice in even the best intentioned schools.

It may be more honest for a school to identify certain times when the headteacher or the class teachers will ensure that they are available, with the offer of appointments at other times. If this is backed up by high quality informal contacts at the class or school door there may actually be more parent-teacher contact than in some schools with "open door" policies. However the contact should not just be left to the parents' initiative. There will be times when the teacher or the headteacher feels that it would be helpful to have a short talk with the parents. This may not be about a problem. There should be no inhibitions about approaching the parent and initiating the discussion; however if the class teacher wishes to discuss difficulties then it is probably wise for her to mention this to the headteacher first, as the head may be aware of problems in the home which could be causing them. Nevertheless the conversation with the parents should go forward. The aim should be to establish an open atmosphere of partnership and mutual trust so that either party can raise difficulties, worries, concerns or joys and successes in the knowledge that the other will be a willing participant in the discussion and that this will express a shared concern for the education of the child.

The annual Parents' Meeting

Each year the Governors of the school must present an annual report about the way in which they have exercised their responsibilities in the school to a meeting of the parents. While this is not the direct responsibility of those teachers who are not members of the governing body, all the staff of the school have an interest in ensuring that this meeting makes its own particular contribution to the relationships between the parents and the school. Teachers may have been asked to make reports to the governing body about one of their areas of special responsibility during the year. If this has happened it is likely that it will be mentioned in the governors' annual report, and the governors may request that the teacher is present at the meeting to answer questions from the parents about this item. However it is more likely that the staff will be invited to attend principally in order to give full expression to the partnership which exists between the governors, the staff and the parents in a Church school. In some quarters these meetings have gained a poor reputation as a result of low attendances. It must be expected that attendances will improve as parents come to see the value of them and they cease to be something new grafted on to the school year and become a significant regular feature of it.

P.T.A.s

In almost all Church schools there will be a formal organisation which gives expression to the partnership between the school, the parents and the wider community. This will often be the parent teacher association, but in some places it will be called the Friends of the school, in order to make clear that members of the Church or wider community that the school serves are welcome to join and play a full role in the activities, even if they do not have a child in attendance at the school. This opportunity for the involvement of the wider community may be particularly important when the school is serving a clearly defined geographical area, or a stable community with strong historic associations with the school. It is for the school to decide which type of organisation is most appropriate to its circumstances, but whatever form it takes it will be important that the staff of the school are seen to be active supporters of it.

No room for suspicion

There still exists in some parts of the teaching profession a suspicion of parents and their motives. There is no room for this in

Church schools. There should be a commitment to developing a partnership with parents for the benefit of the children's education. This partnership should be based on a gospel inspired view of the way in which human relationships should be conducted. Of course this is not easy, but attempting to build relationships at this level never is, as St Paul's letters so often remind us. The rewards in terms of the children's learning however and the teachers' professional fulfilment are worth the effort that it takes.

Questions for reflection and discussion

1. How can a school enable nervous parents to became partners in their child's education?
2. Are there circumstances when the offer from parents of help in the school should be rejected? How could this be done without damaging the relationship with those parents?

10

How a Church School is Managed

Governing bodies

> In a Church school the governors with two exceptions were not well known to the staff. The first of these two was the parish priest; the other was an elderly retired teacher. She rarely spoke in the governors' meetings, and was occasionally known to fall asleep during the duller bits of the agenda. However she came to every school activity to which she was invited and always had a word or two with the teachers.

The governing body of a Church primary school has been subject to as much review and new legislation in the past few years as have the teachers. Aided and Special Agreement school governing bodies have been reconstituted once and Controlled school governor bodies twice. The powers and responsibilities have increased, as has the work load. There have been greatly increased opportunities for governors to obtain training. This has meant that there are many new governors and a number of old ones who find themselves uncertain of what they are supposed to be doing. Is it still acceptable for them to sleep through the meetings but to be an understanding friend to the staff, or is more now expected? What about teacher governors? How is the work of the governing body of a Church school distinguished from that of a county school. In order to clarify some aspects of this it is worth considering some of the functions of the governing body as they relate to the management of the school.

Finance

Dear Parents,

As part of the fund-raising efforts to pay our share of the costs of the new hall the headteacher is going to undertake a sponsored walk with his son. They are intending to spend a week in the Lake District fell walking, and they are asking people to sponsor them on the basis of the number of peaks that they will climb in seven days. They hope to cover fifty three. If you would like to sponsor them please fill in the enclosed form.

All governing bodies are now responsible for the finances delegated to them by the Local Education Authority to enable them to manage the school. There will be budgets to prepare, and some difficult decisions to make. In approaching these the governors will be guided by the school development plan which they have helped to draw up and which they have approved. The staff will also have had an input into the development plan, but it is the governors who have the responsibility for its policies. A well constructed plan will assist the governors in preparing the budget for the school and in balancing conflicting demands for resources. Every teacher will have proposals that they will wish to see included in the budget, particularly if they have responsibility for the leadership of a curriculum area. Part of the teachers' task will be to make a case for their ideas, to argue for it and then to accept the decision when it has been made. If the decision is positive they may then have the challenge of ensuring that the financial allocation has been properly spent and that it produces the benefits which were claimed for it when the case was made. In a well organised school, every teacher will be expected to accept some responsibility for an aspect of the budget, and this will grow as the teacher develops experience and demonstrates the necessary management ability. Clearly in all the discussion that centres round financial questions there are two principles which should be observed in Church schools. The first is absolute honesty and straightforward dealing with regard to money, and the second is that respect and careful attention should be given to everyone who is participating in the debate on how the money should be spent.

Policy

The wife of a former colleague used to take the football in the primary school at which she taught. She did not know all the rules, and therefore she adopted two guiding principles.

1. The field of play is limited, and these limits are where the referee says they are.

2. Players kick the ball and not each other.

My colleague would often quote these two rules before any debate was initiated in which he knew that opinions were passionately held.

Every school will have a range of policy documents, most of which will relate to the school development plan. These are the policies of the governors, and as such will have been debated and approved by them. They will include policies on all the traditional curriculum areas, as well as sex education, equal opportunities and other matters that affect the running of the school. The teachers' role in the development and delivery of these policies is very important. The teaching staff form a major professional resource to advise and help the governors formulate the policies. All teachers will be expected to take part in the discussions that lead to the review of existing policies and the development of new ones. When these have been debated in the governing body and approved it will then be the responsibility of the teachers to implement the policy in the best interests of the children. Some teachers with a particular interest or responsibility in an area of the curriculum may be asked to present papers to the governing body on their subject. All teachers may find themselves asked to work with governors on some topics. Such debates require from teachers a high level of professional integrity and flexibility, as they need to be prepared to justify their views on professional matters in ways which communicate to non-professionals, and which do not rest on undisclosed professional assumptions about the nature of teaching or a particular topic. Within a Church school there will be many occasions when a spiritual and theological understanding will underpin the policy adopted alongside educational, philosophical and sociological frameworks. Some of the topics likely to be affected in this way have already been mentioned in earlier chapters.

Buildings

> One quiet day I was sitting in my office preparing the next term's programme of worship when I received a phone call from a colleague. "David, the Area Education Office has suggested that I contact you. We have been having some trouble with our drains. They keep blocking. They told me to talk to you about it, because you are so good with yours." I thought to myself, "Here at last is the professional recognition that I craved. I would rather have been known for my expertise as a developer of the curriculum, but one must accept the judgement of the world. At least I am known to be good at something."

The governors of all schools have a responsibility for the buildings, including the health and safety of those within them. In Aided schools this extends to having to raise some of the finance to keep them in good condition and to develop them to meet new demands or standards. In all schools the maintenance of the building is within the governors' responsibility either through the delegated budget from the Local Education Authority or from their own funds grant aided by the Department of Education and Science. Teachers have a responsibility to assist the governors in this task. It will not be everyone's lot to clear blocked drains before the nursery class arrives for school in the morning (which was how my reputation for being good with drains was created). Indeed the circumstances that led to that situation were happily exceptional. However every teacher can seek to ensure that the children respect the buildings that they are in, and as a result do not cause anything other than normal wear and tear.

Equally teachers must observe any safety rules, and ensure that their children do so. If the maintenance costs of a building are high the budget available for other educational purposes will have to be reduced correspondingly. Thus there is a direct potential benefit to teachers if they are effective in encouraging care for the building. There is also an issue of care for the world's resources to which all concerned with the school will be sensitive. The Bible teaches us that we are to be good stewards of the world. We can reflect this in our care for the buildings in which we work. Well cared for buildings are also more pleasant to work in, and therefore there are benefits to all in ensuring that proper care is taken.

This does not imply that teachers are being asked to keep poorly maintained buildings going regardless of their state. What is needed is sensible budgeted expenditure to maintain the building well.

Staffing

The interviews for the post of headteacher of the Church school were scheduled to last the whole day. At lunch time the candidates and the governors shared a buffet lunch provided by the conference centre where the interviews were being held. Two of the candidates were looking at a plate of canapes which included some biscuits with what looked like small black lead shot on them.

"What's that?" asked one.

"I think it's caviar," said the other, and ate one of the biscuits. "Yes it is, delicious."

Someone must have been taking notes. The candidate who recognised the caviar was duly appointed to the post in the afternoon.

Aided school governors have always been the employers of the staff, and increasingly the governors of Controlled schools are taking on many of the same responsibilities. At the moment the Local Education Authorities are still the paymasters, but even this pattern is now subject to some change. As a result all Church school governing bodies now have policies on a number of staffing matters, and their own procedures, probably agreed in consultation with the diocese and the Local Education Authority. They will have their own approach to interviewing, to staff grievances and discipline and to staff development. Every teacher in a Church school should be aware of these. Many will be outlined in the contract of employment which the teacher signs with the governors.

Such policies will reflect not only the legal requirements, but also the governors' understanding of what it means to be a Church school. Clearly there will be some differences between what is acceptable in a Church school and what is acceptable in a county school. This will include the fact that teachers must be prepared to assent to and work within a framework of policy which reflects many of the issues addressed in this book. Teachers who are unable to do this should probably look for a move to a school where the philosophy does not cause them to have such crises of conscience. In most county schools there is no overt concern amongst the governing body for the teacher's "private" life. This can not always be true in a Church school. A teacher who chooses to teach in a Church school has to accept that if the situation arose that their home life became a matter of public knowledge and was perceived to be conducted in a way that was clearly against the teaching of the school, and was therefore undermining it, the governors would have to take action to protect the school.

However it is not only the rare problems and difficulties with which the governors are concerned, they are also involved in the positive aspects of the employment of staff. They will be committed to encouraging the development of further professional skills amongst the teachers and with issues that affect teacher morale. These may include the facilities in the staff room and the arrangements for lunch time supervision of the children. They will also be positive in their support for activities that tend to build co-operation within the staff team.

So far this chapter has looked at some of the areas of the governing body's work as it may impinge on the role of the teacher in a Church school. It is now important to turn to individuals or groups of people within the management structure of the school, and consider their role.

The parish priest

Earlier chapters have considered the role of the parish priest in supporting the curriculum of the school and as a resource for the worship. He will also be a member of the governing body unless he has chosen not to be so. As such he is in the position to make a major contribution to the spiritual insight that the governors will need in order to conduct their affairs. As a result of the knowledge that he has of the school, it can also be assumed that his contribution will be significant across a wide range of their work. He is likely to be a member of most interviewing panels, and to be a representative of the governors at meetings about the school. If he has more than one Church school in his parish, they are likely to take up a considerable amount of his time. There is a strong tradition within Church circles that the incumbent is the chairman of governors. This is not automatic, as there is no legal reason why the governors should not elect another of their members to chair their meetings. Indeed there are some incumbents who feel that the role of chairman of governors may conflict with their role as chaplain to the school and its staff. Where this is the case they are often active in seeking to find one of the other governors to take on the role of chairman.

The chair of governors

There seems to be no universally accepted word to indicate that it is understood that the person taking the chair at the governors' meeting can be either female or male, but it is clear that apart from the tradition mentioned in the preceding paragraph the only criterion which will be applied by the governing body in the election of someone to take the chair will be their fitness for the post and their ability to give the time to the task that it requires. The task of the chairman is a demanding one as they will need to be able to give time to visit the school, talk to the head and the staff, attend meetings, not only of the governing body, but also with Local Education Authority or diocesan officers, and read the papers that have been prepared for the meetings. They also need as clear an understanding of the aims of the school as the headteacher, in order that they can provide guidance to the governors and the head about the way in which issues under discussion affect or are affected by the Christian foundation of the school.

The teacher governors

Teacher governors are full members of the governing body, and should participate in all aspects of the work of the governors. The only limit on this is that they should not participate in staff matters including appointments where they could be understood to have a potential personal benefit from the outcome. They are not elected onto the governing body to be a watchdog on behalf of the staff, any more than the parent or foundation governors are there to play that role on behalf of those who elect or nominate them. However there will be an expectation that their professional knowledge and their knowledge of their colleagues' attitudes will be a significant part of their contribution to the work of the governors.

All teachers in Church schools should take seriously the process of electing a teacher governor, and be prepared to undertake the task if it is their colleagues' wish that they do so. It can be an interesting and potentially fulfilling professional role. The teacher governor will need to develop a good relationship with the headteacher in order to ensure that there are no mis-understandings between them about their roles on the governing body or in the school.

The parents

For schools which take seriously their partnership with the parents in offering education to their children the role of the parents on the governing body will be natural and obvious. In the first instance it gives tangible expression to the partnership that exists at this, as at all other levels of the school's organisation. In Aided schools some of the parent governors will be elected, others will be nominated by the foundation. In Controlled schools all the parent governors will be elected. Once they are members of the governing body they will contribute to the meetings, decisions and general work of the governors in the same ways that other governors do. They also have a particular responsibility to play their part in developing and maintaining good relationships between the school and the parents. This does not make them watchdogs or guardians of the parents' interests any more than other governors are, it simply ensures that there are governors who are well placed to contribute to good communication with parents.

The foundation governors

These are governors who are nominated by the Church, usually some by the local parish directly and some in consultation with the diocese. In an Aided school or a Special Agreement school they will be in a majority over all other categories of governors. In a Controlled school the foundation governors form one group among many, none of whom have a majority. For most purposes there is no difference between foundation governors and others, and all governors should be working together for the good of the school. There are one or two issues on which it should be expected that foundation governors will have a particularly keen interest, and occasionally there are technical matters in which they have special responsibilities. These issues will include the relationship with the parish church, the quality of the Religious Education and Worship in the school and the basic understandings that support the ethos of the school.

The headteacher

The headteacher has responsibility for the day to day running of the school in accordance with the policies of the governing body. He or she will have been the principal adviser to the governors on those policies when they were being determined, and will probably initiate any review of them. This implies that the role of headteacher is, despite the increase in the role of the governors, still the key one in determining the success or failure of the school. Attempts to circumvent this have always foundered on the need for clear direction and good management. It is the headteacher who will set the principal example in terms of the human relations within the school, and also in terms of the way in which spiritual and theological insights affect the way in which the school is run. In this they are entitled to expect that the teachers in the school will endeavour to follow their lead and support them in their approach.

The headteacher of a Church school had reached the end of his patience with a member of staff who was constantly late arriving at school, and who failed to prepare his work adequately. He decided that it would be necessary to give him a formal verbal warning. Therefore he called the teacher into his room and explained what he was going to do and why. The teacher's comment was, "Can't we handle this like Christians?"

There are those who think that adopting a Christian attitude simply means turning the other cheek and always trying to be gentle and avoid giving offence. Perhaps the lazy teacher in this anecdote thought that. This is only part of the gospel. As teachers we are given the task of providing a good education for the children entrusted to us. In a Church school this will be informed by Christian principles. If we fail in this trust then we must expect to be called to account. This is clearly in parallel with our attitude to the discipline of children.

Christians are called to witness to the redeeming love of Christ. This witness is best demonstrated when sin is challenged in ways that make it clear that there is forgiveness and reconciliation available for those who acknowledge that sin, are sorry and want to do something about it. This is where those who think that you can go straight from sin to reconciliation miss the point. Sin has consequences, and there has to be action to put things right.

This is not the only principle on which a Church school will manage its affairs. It will also be seeking to reflect the love of God for each human being, the responsibility to be good stewards of resources that are in our care, a delight in beauty, order and goodness and a straightforward honesty in dealings with others. It is the task of those involved in the management of the school to ensure that their actions and policies are informed by these insights.

Questions for reflection and discussion

1. Are there limits to honesty and openness in the management of a Church school? What place is there for confidences?
2. Are strong management style and a commitment to the Christian gospel compatible in school leadership?

11

Teaching in a Church School

Striving for a good education

The room shared by the three classes covering years two to six was an Aladdin's cave of art work in two and three dimensions. Everywhere you looked there was high quality work on display. All the wall space had long been occupied so there were strings of pictures across the room. There were models here and sculptures there. One end of the room was entirely given over to a picture of an Amazonian rain forest. At the other end were the details of some experiments on different materials. In the middle the children were putting the final touches to a display on re-cycling packaging that was to be mounted opposite the check-out of the local supermarket. Yesterday the cameras had been in from a local television station's news magazine programme to record the work and some of the children's comments. The headteacher was talking to me about her school.

"Well," she said, "I don't suppose that we are very different from any other school, but we do enjoy ourselves here."

You may think that it sounds a bit more than just an ordinary Church school, as indeed it is. It does reflect some of the characteristics that many Church schools will be striving for. There was a lively atmosphere in which children were enjoying their learning, and which the staff also enjoyed. There was an appreciation of beauty, but also an acknowledgement of the ugliness that is in the world. There was an attempt not only to teach the children but also to enable them to share their learning with others, and in the process perhaps do something about some of the darker parts of our experience. There was hard work in plenty and there was also not a little inspiration. All these things should be a feature of every classroom in a Church school.

We must take the first two sections of part one of the Education Reform Act 1988 seriously. It is these paragraphs that discuss the importance of the spiritual, moral, cultural, mental and physical development of pupils in the context of a balanced and broadly based curriculum, which is more than just the subjects in the National Curriculum. Throughout this book there has been a concern to work these issues into every aspect of the work of the teacher in a Church school, in ways which represent good practice and take account of the imperatives of the Gospel.

Sharing the joys and the sorrows

The curriculum is of course more than just the subjects and topics that are taught. It consists of everything that the children learn. Perhaps the greatest crime within this total curriculum is that it should be bland. There must be room for enthusiasm, joy, sadness, anger, cynicism, and laughter.

> We all knew that Kelly's mum was dying. The children in Kelly's class, year six, were aware of it and all the staff who had seen her at the last open evening knew that she could not sustain her long battle with cancer much longer. One day Kelly was not in school and soon after we received the news that her mum was dead. It seemed right to tell the class, and so their teacher gave them the news. There were some tears, and then some talk about it. Then came the reflection that perhaps we could be sad with Kelly, but that if her mum was not hurting any more then perhaps there was also something good in this death. Later the class also talked about how they could help and support Kelly when she returned to school or when they met her in the street.

Fred was in year six and possessed an engagingly cynical view of the world. Every Christmas as part of the Christmas celebrations Father Christmas visited the school and gave each child a small present. These gifts were individually named to ensure that no-one missed out. This year, years five and six, some seventy children in all, were in the hall when Father Christmas arrived. With much ceremony he opened his sack and began to give out the presents. Fred sidled up to me.

"Here, where did you get him from then?"

I do not know why my reply was, "Those who don't believe, Fred...."

"Oh," he said.

He waited. Gifts came out of the sack, but not his. He began to be slightly uncomfortable. He waited some more. The sack was nearly empty. At last, sixty-ninth out of the seventy presents, came Fred's. You could hear his sigh of relief all across the hall.

For many teachers and governors there seems to be the feeling that the well ordered school is the school in which everything proceeds at a calm orderly even tenor with no ripples of laughter or tears to disturb the mood. If such a school were to be achievable it would be a dull place, and some of the most important lessons would never be learned. How can you learn empathy if you never feel like weeping with those who weep or rejoicing with those who rejoice. Likewise it will be important that children have the opportunity to learn both to succeed and to fail in an environment in which they are helped to handle both experiences.

The importance of the teacher

The teachers in a Church school are the key adults who have to take on the challenge of achieving all of this. They must be well-read enthusiastic professionals, with a clear understanding of what their task is and how they are going to tackle it. They must be able to commit themselves to doing this in the context of a Church school which has at its heart the Gospel of Christ. Does this mean that they must all be committed Christians? If this demand were enforced the Church schools would lose many very good teachers, and so the answer has to be no. However they must be able to work within an overtly Christian framework. At the least this implies that they are concerned about spiritual matters, and know what they do believe. On the other hand the governors of a Church school would find it very difficult to sustain the Christian nature of the school if the proportion of teachers who were committed Christians fell. Therefore in any Church school there is likely to be a proportion, and possibly a high proportion of the teachers who are committed Christians, working alongside colleagues who are not able to make that commitment, but who are comfortable and, hopefully, pleased to be working within an atmosphere which is generated by it. Naturally in seeking to ensure the balance governors will tend to look for explicit commitment from the more senior members of the staff, because of their clear leadership roles.

Apart from their faith and their professionalism, the children also need something else from their teachers. They deserve teachers who are lively, interesting and interested human beings. A teacher who does nothing but work and go to Church will be in danger of becoming rather dull. There needs to be time for all teachers to pursue their own interests, so that they continue to grow, and so that the children can come into contact with their teachers' enthusiasms. We may wish to teach our children that commitment to learning as a life-long process is vital. It is much more effective if we show them. This is the point of having times of quiet reading in the classroom when the teacher reads a book as well as the children, but it must go further than this. The children should come to know that Mr Smith is involved in amateur theatre, or that Miss Jones is a mountaineer.

The teacher of the reception class had, with her husband, purchased an old bungalow with a large garden. They spent nearly two years building themselves a new house in the garden of their bungalow, and when they moved in they then demolished the old bungalow, and turned the space into a garden. When year five were doing some investigation into building materials the reception teacher was persuaded to visit the class and tell them about what she had been doing. Not only did it develop the children's understanding of the topic that they were studying, it also contributed significantly to the equal opportunities education work of the school, as the children heard about her experience of brick laying.

The vocation of the teacher

Teachers have to be paragons of virtue, capable of tireless work and endlessly patient. They have to be enthusiasts, committed to education and to the spiritual quest and able communicators. The demands that we make are legion. The rewards are inevitably too small, but teachers are entitled to respect and support from the parents the public at large and from the Church. There is no more challenging vocation, and the Church must support those who willingly respond to it.

There have been a number of very rewarding experiences within my own teaching career. Amongst these was the family in which the mother and three children were all baptised together as a result of contact with my Church school. However perhaps amongst the highest moments was watching an ex-pupil play in a Wembley Cup Final. I had nurtured his talent for the game through the school team and on into the borough's representative side, and here he was fulfilling the highest ambition of most footballers. To complete the triumph of the day, he was to go on to get a winner's medal.

Alas, as a primary teacher, I had also taught him English. Hearing him respond in the standard footballer cliches, such as "Well, I'm just happy to be part of it, i'n't I, Bob?", when interviewed before the match, was to understand that success and failure are but two sides of the same coin.

NOTES

Chapter 1 What is a Church School?
1. Leslie J. Francis, *Partnership in Rural Education* (Collins, 1986)
2. *DES Statistical Summaries 1991* (DES, 1991)
3. *All God's Children?: Children's Evangelism in Crisis* (NS/CHP, 1991)
4. *The Fourth R: The Durham Report on Religious Education* (NS/SPCK, 1970)
5. *A Future in Partnership* (National Society, 1984)
6. *To a Rebellious House* (CIO, 1981)

Chapter 3 The Curriculum
1. Paul Hirst ,"Christian education: a contradiction in terms?", *Learning for Living*, 11(4), 1972, 6-11; "Education, catechesis and the Church School", *British Journal of Religious Education*, 3, 1981, 85-93
2. Dummett and McNeal, *Race and Church Schools* (Runnymede Trust, 1981)

Chapter 5 Integration and Balance in the Curriculum
1. David Hay, "The bearing of empirical studies of religious experience on education", *Research Papers in Education*, 5(1), 1990, 3-28

The National Society

The National Society (Church of England) for Promoting Religious Education is the charity, founded in 1811, which established the first network of schools in England and Wales based on the National Church. It now supports all those involved in Christian education – diocesan education teams, teachers, governors, clergy, students and parents – with the resources of its RE Centres, archives, courses and conferences. The Society publishes a wide range of books, pamphlets and audio-visual items and two magazines, **Crosscurrent** and **Together**. It can give legal and administrative advice for schools and colleges and award grants for church school building projects.

The Society works in close association with the General Synod Board of Education, and with the Division for Education of the Church in Wales, but greatly values the independent status which enables it to take initiatives in developing new work. The Society has a particular concern for Christian goals and values in education as a whole.

For details of corporate, associate and individual membership of the Society contact: The Promotions Secretary, The National Society, Church House, Great Smith Street, London SW1P 3NZ. Telephone 071-222 1672.